EMERGING TECHNOLOGIES IN LAW PRACTICE

MATTHEW N. O. SADIKU, PH.D., P.E.

REGENTS PROFESSOR EMERITUS AND IEEE LIFE FELLOW
PRAIRIE VIEW A&M UNIVERSITY
PRAIRIE VIEW, TX 77446
EMAIL: SADIKU@IEEE.ORG
WEB: WWW.MATTHEW-SADIKU.COM

BOOK FILMS MEDIA

Date published: March 07, 2025

Matthew N. O. Sadiku
sadiku@ieee.org
www.matthew-sadiku.com

Paperback: 978-1-967753-25-3
eBook: 978-1-967753-26-0
Hardcover: 978-1-967753-27-7

BookFilmsMedia
2780 South Jones Blvd Suite 200 - 4007
Las Vegas, NV 89146 United States
+1 725 - 238 - 6534

Photo in Cover: Dan Faggella, Nov. 28, 2017
https://emerj.com/ai-in-law-legal-practice-current-applications/

DEDICATED TO MY WIFE:

JANET O. SADIKU

BRIEF TABLE OF CONTENTS

PREFACE

The legal field is continually evolving, adapting to the changes brought about by technology. As courtroom technology evolves, legal professionals need tools that can keep up. Technology is vital in law for enhancing efficiency, benefiting both legal professionals and clients. It is driving innovation in legal services, leading to new ways of delivering legal assistance. Emerging technologies such as artificial intelligence (AI), blockchain, and cloud computing are reshaping industries, including the legal industry. When adopted strategically and implemented right, emerging technologies transform the ways the companies in the legal industry operate daily.

Organizations of all sizes rely on a variety of tools and technologies to function and compete in today's digital world. With the growing world and its technology, it is important for law firms to adopt new ways to deal with the competition. In an era dominated by digital advancements, many legal practices have embraced technology to streamline operations, enhance efficiency, and facilitate better communication.

This book explores emerging technologies used in law practice. It is organized into 10 chapters that summarize emerging law technologies: artificial intelligence, cloud computing, blockchain, legal automation, virtual legal assistant, immersive technologies, litigation management, identity management, and cybersecurity.

Chapter 1 - Introduction:

This chapter examines the impact of emerging technologies in legal practice and serves as introduction to the entire book. Emerging technology is a term generally used to describe new technology. Emerging technologies are shaping our societies.

They continue to affect the way we live, work, and interact with one another. The legal profession and the future law firm will be radically different as a result of the advancement of technology.

Chapter 2 - Artificial Intelligence:

This chapter discusses how and why corporate legal departments are embracing artificial intelligence (AI) in their complex legal practice. AI refers to the development of computer systems that can perform tasks that typically require human intelligence, such as learning, reasoning, perception, and decision-making. The goal of AI is to create intelligent machines that can perform tasks more efficiently, accurately, and autonomously than humans. AI is transforming the legal industry for lawyers, the courtroom, consumers, education, and the future of law practice. There is clearly great promise in what AI tools can and will do to support legal professionals in their work. AI will create new opportunities for the legal profession.

Chapter 3 - Legal Automation:

In this chapter, we will examine how automation is being applied in different legal practice areas. By nature, legal work has always been document-heavy, detail-oriented, and time-sensitive. Many legal professionals find themselves bogged down by repetitive tasks that could be handled more efficiently with technology. Legal automation simplifies time-consuming tasks, giving lawyers more time to focus on higher-value work. The firms that proactively integrate legal automation into their processes will gain a strategic edge in an industry that is increasingly digital. Automation is not here to replace lawyers; it is here to make them more effective.

Chapter 4 - Virtual Legal Assistant:

This chapter examines how virtual legal assistants improve productivity and free up legal professionals to concentrate on what they do best. It is hard for a law firm to handle all the legal affairs by itself. Having administrative support can make the difference between being ready for your next case and becoming overburdened. More and more law firms are choosing virtual legal assistants to handle these routine but essential tasks. A virtual legal assistant

(VLA) is a skilled professional who provides remote assistance to legal practitioners and law firms. Virtual legal assistants (VLAs) are responsible for handling repetitive but essential tasks, such as transcription, file management, legal research, email and call handling, and client . They are reshaping the legal landscape by helping firms gain a competitive edge, streamline workflows, and offer more personalized services to their clients scheduling.

Chapter 5 - Cloud Computing:

This chapter considers how cloud computing is revolutionizing legal practice. Cloud computing is a computing paradigm for delivering computing services (such as servers, storage, databases, networking, software, analytics, and more) over the "the cloud" with pay-as-you-go pricing. It is a means of pooling and sharing hardware and software resources on a massive scale. Cloud computing in law refers to the legal framework and regulations governing the use of cloud services, encompassing data privacy, security, intellectual property, and jurisdictional issues. The technology has allowed law offices to increase efficiency, streamline workflows, collaborate seamlessly with clients globally, and access resources from anywhere at any time.

Chapter 6 - Immersive Technologies:

The purpose of this chapter is to explore the impact of immersive technologies on law practice. Immersive technologies essentially consist in adding virtual objects to the real world and are mainly virtual reality and augmented reality. Virtual reality immerses viewers in a virtual environment while augmented reality overlays digital visuals on real-world objects. While immersive technologies in law practice are still evolving, their potential to revolutionize how lawyers interact with clients, collaborate globally, and offer more accessible legal services is significant. Immersive technologies will become more accessible to law firms and courts of all sizes.

Chapter 7 - Blockchain:

The objective of this chapter is to explore the integration of blockchain into the legal profession. Blockchain is a distributed ledger system for recording and storing transactions. Integrating the legal industry with blockchain technology will offer a higher level of precision. By offering a decentralized and secure method of recording transactions, blockchain is fundamentally transforming how legal transactions are handled. In the foreseeable future, blockchain may change how law firms conduct a multitude of services.

Chapter 8 - Litigation Management:

This chapter is intended to be a definitive resource for litigation management. Litigation is the process by which the legal system attempts to resolve disputes. Litigation management refers to the coordinated approach to overseeing and directing all phases of a lawsuit or legal dispute, from the beginning through to its resolution. The primary goal of litigation management is to ensure that legal disputes are handled in an organized, efficient, and effective manner. It often boils down to lawyer management.

Chapter 9 - Identity Management:

In this chapter, we will explore the role of identity management solutions in securing users and devices. In the era of digital transformation, digital identity management emerges as a key enabler for organizations seeking to enhance cybersecurity, strengthen customer trust, and comply with regulatory requirements. Evolving cyber threats have increased the risk of online identities becoming compromised and traditional user authentication methods (using username and password, biometrics, etc.) have proven to be lacking. Identity management refers to how an organization identifies and authenticates individuals for access to its networks or applications. Effective digital identity management provides personal protection by verifying that users are who they claim to be through strong authentication methods.

Chapter 10 - Cybersecurity:

This chapter aims to explore the complex landscape of cybersecurity in the legal industry. Cybersecurity is the protection of systems and information connected to the Internet. It remains a top concern in the legal profession. Lawyers are entrusted with sensitive information, making them prime targets for cyber threats. Hackers are increasingly targeting law firms because they can become a one-stop shop for a variety of sensitive documents and a gold mine of information. Cybersecurity and data protection have become a critical aspect of the legal profession since lawyers are bound by various laws and regulations that mandate the protection of their client data. By taking proactive steps, legal practitioner can significantly reduce the risk of a cyberattack and ensure that your data remains secure.

This book is a comprehensive text on the emerging technologies in law practice. It provides an overview of each emerging technology in a way that beginners can understand. It is a must read for those interested in law practice and its future.

— M. N. O. Sadiku

ABOUT THE AUTHOR

Matthew N. O. Sadiku received his B. Sc. degree in 1978 from Ahmadu Bello University, Zaria, Nigeria and his M.Sc. and Ph.D. degrees from Tennessee Technological University, Cookeville, TN in 1982 and 1984 respectively. From 1984 to 1988, he was an assistant professor at Florida Atlantic University, Boca Raton, FL, where he did graduate work in computer science. In total, he received seven college degrees. From 1988 to 2000, he was at Temple University, Philadelphia, PA, where he became a full professor. From 2000 to 2002, he was with Lucent/Avaya, Holmdel, NJ as a system engineer and with Boeing Satellite Systems, Los Angeles, CA as a senior scientist. He is presently a Regents professor emeritus of electrical and computer engineering at Prairie View A&M University, Prairie View, TX.

He is the author of over 1,450 professional papers and over 150 books including "Elements of Electromagnetics" (Oxford University Press, 7th ed., 2018), "Fundamentals of Electric Circuits" (McGraw-Hill, 7th ed., 2020, with C. Alexander), "Computational Electromagnetics with MATLAB" (CRC Press, 4th ed., 2019), "Principles of Modern Communication Systems" (Cambridge University Press, 2017, with S. O. Agbo), and "Emerging Internet-based Technologies" (CRC Press, 2019). In addition to the engineering books, he has written Christian books including "Secrets of Successful Marriages" (with J. O. Sadiku), "How to Discover God's Will for Your Life," and commentaries on all the books of the New Testament Bible. Some of his books have been translated into ten languages: French, Korean, Chinese (and Chinese Long Form in Taiwan), Italian, Portuguese, Spanish, German, Dutch, Polish, and Russian.

He was the recipient of the 2000 McGraw-Hill/Jacob Millman Award for outstanding contributions in the field of electrical engineering. He was also the recipient of Regents Professor award for 2012-2013 by the Texas A&M University System. He is a registered professional engineer and a life fellow of the Institute of Electrical and Electronics Engineers (IEEE) "for contributions to computational electromagnetics and engineering education." He was the IEEE Region 2 Student Activities Committee Chairman. He was an associate editor for IEEE Transactions on Education. He is also a member of Association for Computing Machinery (ACM). His current research interests are in the areas of computational electromagnetic, computer science/networks, engineering education, and marriage counseling. His works can be found in his autobiography, "My Life and Work" (Trafford Publishing, 2024) or his website: www.matthew-sadiku.com. He can be reached via email at sadiku@ieee.org

TABLE OF CONTENTS

CHAPTER 1
INTRODUCTION

"The intersection of law, politics, and technology is going to force a lot of good thinking."

—Bill Gates

1.1 INTRODUCTION

Technology is vital in law for enhancing efficiency, accuracy, and accessibility, enabling faster research, streamlined workflows, and improved communication, ultimately benefiting both legal professionals and clients. It is driving innovation in legal services, leading to new ways of delivering legal assistance. Emerging technologies such as artificial intelligence (AI), blockchain, the Internet of things (IoT), big data, and cloud computing are reshaping industries, including the legal industry. Emerging technologies are significantly reshaping the legal landscape, creating opportunities and challenges. They automate operations, enhance workflows, and offer new perspectives through data analysis, potentially improving legal services.

In an industry that stands for justice and fairness, the latest technology provides lawyers and attorneys with the tools needed to uphold the rule of law, protect individual rights, and ensure access to justice for all. When adopted strategically and implemented right, emerging technologies transform the ways the companies in the legal industry operate daily. The concepts of legal tech and law tech are related as shown in Figure 1.1 [1].

Legal Tech vs Law Tech

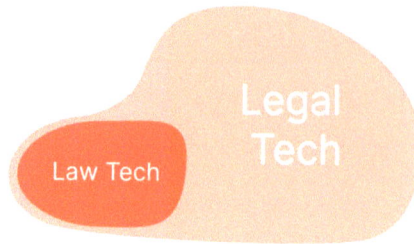

Figure 1.1 The relationship between the concepts of legal tech and law tech [1].

Legal tech generally refers to technology solutions and innovations designed to improve and streamline various processes within the legal industry. Law tech includes technology solutions that impact the practice of law as well as the delivery of legal services.

Emerging technologies are rapidly transforming the legal field in areas like document review, contract management, and client interaction, offering increased efficiency and access to justice. From artificial intelligence to blockchain, emerging technologies promise to revolutionize industries and drive innovation. More than ever, law firms are now leveraging technology advancements to increase efficiency, optimize their bottom line, and improve client satisfaction. The emerging technologies such as artificial intelligence (AI), blockchain, the Internet of things (IoT), big data, and cloud computing are set to have a huge impact on the legal environment. They have ushered in a revolution among industries, especially the legal industry. They are reshaping the world and the practice of law at large [2].

In this chapter, we examine the impact of emerging technologies in legal practice. The chapter begins with explaining what emerging technologies are. It discusses the relationship between technology and legal profession. It covers emerging technologies in law. It highlights the benefits and challenges of emerging technologies in law practice. The last section concludes with comments.

1.2 WHAT ARE EMERGING TECHNOLOGIES?

Technology may be regarded as a collection of systems designed to perform some function. It can help alleviate some of the challenges facing business today. Emerging technology is a term generally used to describe new technology. The term often refers to technologies currently developing or expected to be available within the next five to ten years. Any imminent, but not fully realized, technological innovations will have some impact on the status quo.

Emerging technologies are shaping our societies. They continue to affect the way we live, work, and interact with one another. Emerging technology (ET) lacks a consensus on what classifies them as "emergent." It is a relative term because one may see a technology as emerging and others may not see it the same way. It is a term that is often used to describe a new technology. A technology is still emerging if it is not yet a "must-have" [3]. An emerging technology is the one that holds the promise of creating a new economic engine and is trans-industrial. ET is used in different areas such as media, healthcare, business, science, education, or defense.

The characteristics of emerging technologies include the following [4]:

- *Novelty:* Emerging technologies are typically new or novel, meaning they have yet to be widely adopted or used. They often represent a significant departure from existing technologies or processes.

- *Potential for Disruption:* Emerging technologies have the potential to disrupt existing markets, industries, or ways of doing things. They may also displace existing businesses or industries.

- *Uncertainty:* Because emerging technologies are still in the early stages of development, there is often a high uncertainty surrounding their future potential and impact. It can be challenging to predict how they will evolve.

- *Rapid Change:* Emerging technologies often evolve rapidly, with new developments and innovations emerging frequently. It can make keeping up with the latest trends and advancements challenging.

- *Interdisciplinary:* Emerging technologies often involve multiple disciplines or fields of study, such as computer science, engineering, and biology. They may require collaboration across different fields and industries to develop their potential fully.

Emerging technologies are worth investigating. They are responsible for developing new products or devices. As emerging technologies continue to evolve, engineering is poised for a transformative future. Emerging technologies have driven innovation and progress in today's rapidly evolving digital landscape. The collective impact of emerging technologies such as artificial intelligence, machine learning, big data, and the Internet of things is undeniably transformative. Some emerging technologies are shown in Figure 1.2 [5].

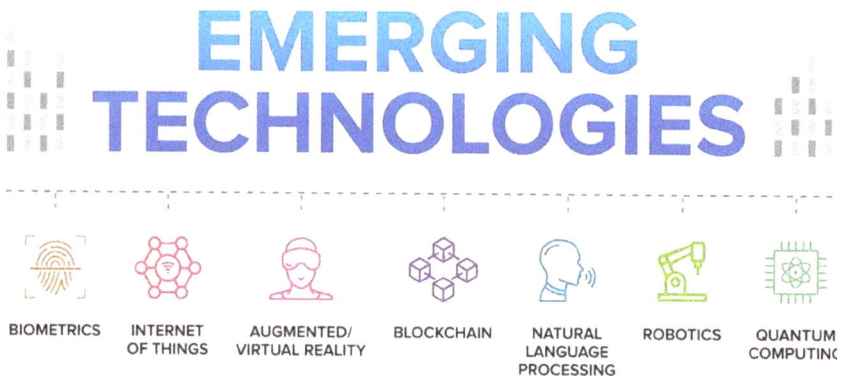

EMERGING TECHNOLOGIES

| BIOMETRICS | INTERNET OF THINGS | AUGMENTED/ VIRTUAL REALITY | BLOCKCHAIN | NATURAL LANGUAGE PROCESSING | ROBOTICS | QUANTUM COMPUTINC |

Figure 1.2 Some emerging technologies [5].

1.3 LEGAL PROFESSION AND TECHNOLOGY

Law is no longer limited to litigation and corporate law. The evolving legal landscape has given rise to several non-traditional career paths for lawyers. The legal field has evolved significantly, becoming one of the most sought-after professions worldwide. The perception of law as a career has shifted dramatically, with increasing numbers of students opting for it over traditional fields like engineering and medicine. One of the key reasons for law's growing popularity is its versatility. Law is not only about courtroom battles and litigations; it is about understanding and interpreting rules and regulations that govern every aspect of life. Entrepreneurs, corporate executives, startups, and established businesses alike rely on lawyers to navigate complex legal landscapes. Lawyers are needed not only in traditional litigation but also in arbitration, mediation, and negotiation. The growing complexity of corporate structures, the proliferation of new industries, and increasing regulatory requirements have made legal expertise indispensable. Whether you are interested in technology-driven legal services, environmental law, corporate law, or public policy, the legal profession offers a diverse range of career paths. Figure 1.3 shows the symbol for legal practice [6], while Figure 1.4 shows a group of lawyers [7].

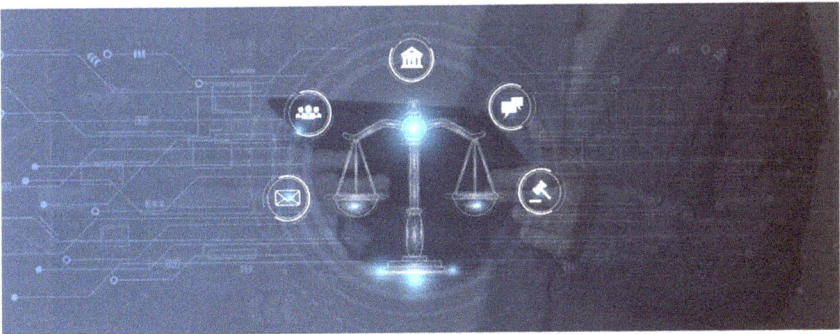

Figure 1.3 Symbol for legal practice [6].

Figure 1.4 A group of lawyers [7].

Technology is revolutionizing the legal profession. The law and technology are constantly evolving in tandem, as new technologies create new legal challenges and opportunities. Digital transformation is sweeping every industry, and with customers moving online, law firms and legal departments have no option but to build and enrich their digital presence. In an industry that is known to be traditional in its working methods, emerging technology trends are bringing about the necessary changes and shaping the modern legal landscape. Although the relationship between law and technology has had a rocky start, technology for lawyers and law firms is now revolutionizing how lawyers and law firms can deliver legal services. Legal technology can streamline legal research by providing access to comprehensive databases of case law, statutes, regulations, and legal commentary, all within a single online platform. Figure 1.5 shows the symbol of technology in law practice [8], while Figure 1.6 shows different components of legal technology [1]. Clients are adopting legal technology at a quicker pace than lawyers and are completing legal tasks on their own to reduce legal fees.

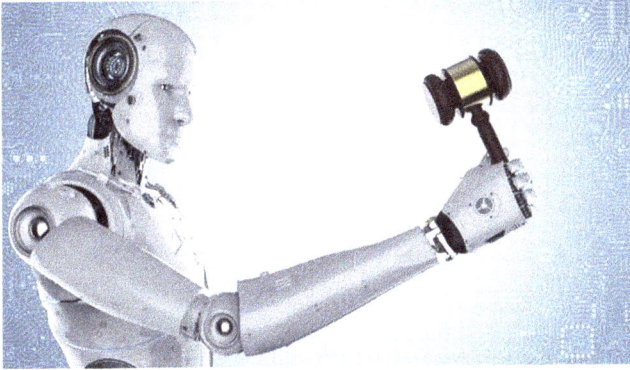

Figure 1.5 Symbol of technology in law practice [8].

Figure 1.6 Components of legal technology [1].

1.4 EMERGING TECHNOLOGIES IN LAW

The legal landscape constantly changes due to technology, client demands, and global shifts. The legal profession is now being disrupted by the advancement of technology. Law firms are under pressure to invest in technological innovation with increased competition in the legal market. The implementation of new technologies, such as artificial intelligence, in the legal field has reduced costs for law firms and improved the speed and accuracy of results while reducing the need for personnel. Emerging technologies are reshaping how the law is practiced and justice is delivered, providing opportunities for increased efficiency, transparency, and accessibility. These emerging technologies include [9]:

1. *Artificial Intelligence:* AI encompasses machine learning, robotics, natural language processing, and expert systems. It is at the forefront of legal innovation, offering capabilities like predictive analytics in case outcomes and automating complex document review processes. It enables automation, data analysis, and decision-making processes across many sectors. It can assist in tasks like contract review and legal research, improving accuracy and identifying potential errors. It can analyze large datasets to identify patterns and predict outcomes, providing valuable insights for legal professionals. AI algorithms can quickly sift through large volumes of documents, identifying relevant information and patterns, freeing up lawyers for more strategic work. AI can automate contract review and analysis, helping to identify potential risks and ensure compliance. AI can be used to analyze crime data and predict potential hotspots, helping law enforcement allocate resources effectively. AI is no longer optional in the legal industry. Generative AI tools like ChatGPT present many opportunities for legal technology entrepreneurs to innovate and develop valuable solutions that streamline workflows, improve decision-making, and drive the evolution of the legal profession. For example, IBM Watson Legal utilizes advanced artificial intelligence and

cognitive computing capabilities to transform legal research and data analysis. Figure 1.7 represents the use of AI in legal field [10].

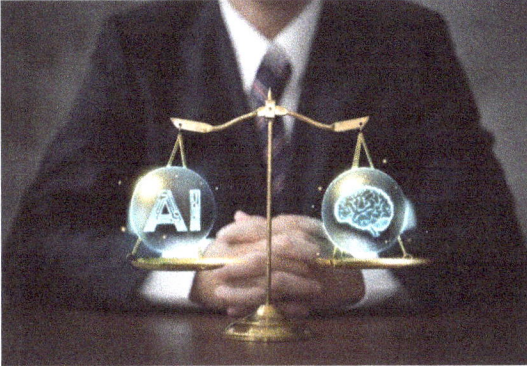

Figure 1.7 Representation of AI in legal field [10].

2. *Automation:* The way lawyers operate is changing due to automation. Automation technology takes over repetitive and time-consuming tasks. Law technology automates routine and repetitive tasks, such as document generation, data entry, document generation, data entry, and scheduling, freeing up lawyers to focus on more complex legal matters. By automating these tasks, law firms can significantly reduce manual labor, mitigate the risk of human errors, and ensure consistency in legal documents and procedures. Automated processes and technology-driven tools reduce the risk of human error in tasks like data entry and document preparation.

3. *Blockchain:* Blockchain technology is also having an impact on the legal industry. Blockchain is a digital ledger that is transparent, secure, and decentralized, enabling smart contract development. Smart contracts are self-executing agreements that automatically enforce their terms when certain conditions are satisfied. Blockchain technology provides a decentralized and secure way to record transactions, offering transparency and immutability. It has applications in finance, supply chain, power systems, and more. Blockchain's decentralized and immutable nature makes it ideal for storing and managing legal records, ensuring authenticity and integrity. Contract talks might be streamlined using this technology, which would also eliminate the need for mediators like attorneys. The use of blockchain for smart

contracts and digital asset management is becoming increasingly popular.

4. *Immersive Technologies:* Virtual reality (VR) and augmented reality (AR) are beginning to make waves in the legal field. These technologies can be used for a variety of applications, such as recreating crime scenes in VR to aid in evidence presentation or employing AR for enhanced document examination. They can be used for training lawyers, simulating courtroom environments, and visualizing complex evidence. VR or AR can help train legal departments by simulating various scenarios and legal environments. Lawyers can also use this legal tech to conduct negotiations without needing to meet face-to-face. VR and online dispute resolution platforms are transforming how disputes are resolved, making the process more efficient and accessible. VR technology can be used to simulate courtroom environments, allowing lawyers and judges to conduct mock trials and practice their skills in a realistic setting. Figure 1.8 shows an example of how immersive technology is used [8].

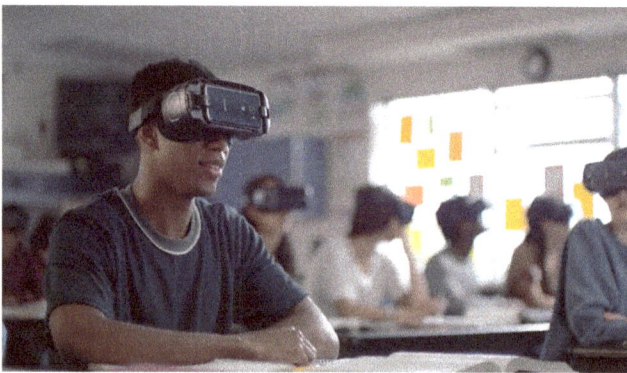

Figure 1.8 An example of how immersive technology is used [8].

5. *Internet of Things (IoT):* IoT connects physical devices to the Internet, allowing for data exchange and automation. IoT devices can generate vast amounts of data that can be used in legal investigations and litigation.

6. *Cybersecurity:* As technology becomes increasingly integrated into the legal field, cybersecurity threats also increase,

requiring legal professionals to be aware of and protect against these risks. Data has become an integral part of legal practice and with the right tools, law firms can encrypt and securely share data within the organization and externally. The increasing interconnectedness of devices and systems through the Internet of things (IoT) and digital platforms creates new opportunities for cybercriminals to exploit vulnerabilities and launch attacks. Cybercriminals exploit the information given to the Internet by the individual and use it for illegal purposes. Legal frameworks governing data security, breach notification, and cybersecurity standards play a vital role in mitigating these risks and protecting sensitive information from unauthorized access, theft, or manipulation.

7. *Cloud Computing:* Cloud-based solutions help lawyers and clients share files and data easily instead of relying solely on emails, improving collaboration and efficiency. The flexibility offered by cloud-based systems facilitates integration between different tools. This allows law firms to effectively manage their practice and bring transparency to communication with each other and clients. Organizations migrating their data to the cloud can enjoy significant benefits.

8. *Litigation Management:* Technological advancements in litigation management software provide comprehensive tools for case management, document storage, and team collaboration. These platforms help achieve a seamless flow of information among legal departments, regardless of geographic location, and enable efficient management of litigation portfolios. It facilitates the discovery process by enabling legal teams to upload, review, and produce documents more efficiently.

9. *Virtual Legal Assistants:* AI-powered technologies called legal chatbots and virtual assistants can help with common legal chores, including booking appointments, responding to frequently requested questions, and even giving preliminary legal advice. Startups and emerging businesses require legal assistance with intellectual property, contract negotiation, and business structuring. Virtual legal assistants (VLAs) are a significant technological advancement in the legal sector, leveraging AI to transform how

law firms interact with their clients. These AI-driven platforms are designed to perform a variety of tasks that traditionally require human intervention, thus optimizing legal operations and improving the client experience. VLAs can manage routine but essential tasks such as scheduling appointments, organizing client meetings, and sending reminders for upcoming deadlines or payments. Chatbots harness the power of deep learning to act as virtual legal assistants (VLAs) to clients. This not only improves response time but frees up resources for high-value tasks. And when the VLAs cannot address a query, they forward it to the concerned department. As they get more sophisticated, VLAs are being implemented by more and larger law firms and organizations.

10. *Identity Management:* This has become a crucial legal tech trend in recent years, emphasizing the secure management of digital identities, sensitive data, and access controls within law firms. By employing advanced solutions that handle user authentication, access rights, and activity monitoring, law firms are better equipped to detect and prevent unauthorized access to legal data. Integrating biometric authentication methods, such as fingerprint scanning and facial recognition, offers a more secure alternative to traditional password systems. For example, Okta offers a comprehensive identity and access management solution tailored for organizations, including law firms.

11. *Smart Legal Contract Management:* This leverages blockchain technology to redefine the dynamics of drafting, executing, and enforcing legal agreements. By embedding contract terms directly into code, smart contracts automate contract negotiation processes when predetermined conditions are met, thereby eliminating the need for manual intervention and making the whole process faster. This legal technology minimizes the ambiguity and disputes that often come with traditional contracts.

1.5 BENEFITS

Understanding the legal implications of emerging technologies is crucial for businesses seeking to leverage these innovations responsibly. Emerging technologies are undoubtedly revolutionizing the practice of law and the delivery of justice. These technologies are designed to augment human capabilities, not replace them. Law firms are focusing on diversity, equity, and inclusion to create a more inclusive work environment. Other benefits include [6]:

- *Client Focus:* Legal industry is moving towards a more client-focused approach with the rest of the business world. Emerging legal technology trends are transforming modern legal practices and shaping the future of the legal industry.

- *Social Media:* Social media has created new ways for people to communicate and share information, but it has also created new legal challenges. As technology continues to change, the law must adapt to ensure that it protects individual rights and freedoms, while also promoting innovation.

- *Environmental Law:* Environmental lawyers are needed to advise companies on how to navigate complex environmental laws and ensure they meet regulatory standards. As the world grapples with climate change and environmental degradation, environmental law is gaining importance. Governments and organizations are enacting strict environmental regulations, creating opportunities for lawyers who specialize in sustainability, renewable energy, and environmental compliance.

- *Paralegals:* In today's rapidly evolving digital age, the role of paralegals is gaining significant importance as law firms recognize the need to adapt to modernize their operations and harness technology for enhanced efficiency. Paralegals play a crucial role in providing an economic advantage to legal practices. They contribute extensively to streamlining legal processes and delivering optimal client experiences. Automation and AI have emerged as prominent trends in the field of paralegal support, revolutionizing the legal world. These technologies have had a profound impact on legal practices, offering unique opportunities for paralegals. Paralegals play a vital role in team collaboration within a law office, working alongside attorneys, legal assistants, and other support staff. Virtual paralegal services offer several benefits, including cost reductions, scalability, and flexibility. To stay competitive in their chosen specialization, paralegals must prioritize professional development and stay abreast of the latest advancements in their field and the legal industry as a whole.

- *Contract Management:* With the help of contract management software, all contracts can be centralized in a digital repository, eliminating the need for manual storage and retrieval of paper documents.

- *Law Enforcement:* The use of new technologies is imperative if the police are going to stay a step ahead of criminals. Along with advanced software, hardware and communications networks, enforcement and investigative tools are becoming increasingly mobile-centric. The idea is to equip officers with the newest and most agile tools so that they can be readily applied in the field. New tools have been introduced to maximize operating efficiency in recent years. These include in-vehicle computers, body cameras, license plate readers, handheld narcotics analyzers, map-based apps, mobile consoles for fingerprint reading, and facial recognition technologies. Figure 1.9 shows a well-equipped officer [11]. It is not just police departments that are using these emerging technological tools. Correctional facilities are now using biometric technologies to improve offender identification and make the employee access authentication more efficient.

Figure 1.9 A well-equipped officer [11].

- *ChatGPT:* ChatGPT, as an advanced AI language model, can be utilized in various aspects of the legal profession. ChatGPT can help lawyers and law students conduct efficient and comprehensive legal research by providing relevant case law, statutes, and regulations based on their queries. It can be used to review and analyze large volumes of documents during the due diligence process, streamlining the workload and reducing the time spent on manual review.

1.6 CHALLENGES

The implementation of cutting-edge technologies in the legal industry is challenging. The legal challenges posed by new technologies are complex and constantly evolving. Irrespective of their type, emerging technologies have serious social implications. They shape our homes, businesses, and governments. For example, there are issues with the precision and dependability of AI-powered legal research tools. While AI tools hold tremendous potential to enhance efficiency, many legal professionals remain hesitant to explore them, representing both a challenge and an opportunity for those ready to adapt. Generative AI is undeniably exciting, but the real challenge for law firms is not adopting new tools; it is reimagining how work gets done within a system that resists change. Other challenges include [12,13]:

- *Data Privacy and Security:* These are paramount in the digital age. Emerging technologies collect and process vast amounts of personal data, raising concerns about how this data is stored, used, and shared. Protecting sensitive data requires robust cybersecurity measures, including encryption, access controls, and regular security audits to prevent data breaches and unauthorized access.

- *Intellectual Property Rights:* These rights are critical for protecting innovations and maintaining a competitive edge. Emerging technologies present unique challenges in IP protection. Choosing the latest emerging technologies with implications for IP is somewhat subjective. Determining ownership and IP rights for AI-generated content, such as art or music, raises questions about authorship and legal protection. Blockchain technology also introduces new forms of IP, such as smart contracts and decentralized applications. In spite of interesting issues across IP, generative AI's implications arguably have been felt most in the copyright realm. Proponents of AI models suggest that copyrighted content is not incorporated verbatim and the content is transformed into something new.

- *Liability:* Determining liability for actions taken by autonomous systems and AI-driven devices is a significant legal challenge. Companies must consider who is liable when an autonomous system causes harm. Is it the manufacturer, the software developer, or the end-user? Developing ethical AI systems also requires addressing biases and ensuring that AI-driven decisions are fair and transparent. Legal standards should define the extent of human involvement required for decision-making.

- *Regulatory Compliance:* Emerging technologies often overshadow existing regulatory frameworks, creating uncertainties and compliance challenges between businesses or individuals and policymakers. Navigating the regulatory landscape for emerging technologies is complex, with industry-specific laws and standards. For example, healthcare technologies must comply with regulations such as the Health Insurance Portability and Accountability Act (HIPAA).

Engaging with regulatory bodies and participating in industry forums can help businesses stay informed about regulatory changes and contribute to shaping industry standards.

- *Ethical Concern:* Technological advancements raise complex ethical questions related to human rights, social justice, and the moral implications of scientific research and innovation. Emerging technologies pose ethical questions that businesses must address to maintain trust, accountability, and credibility. AI algorithms, for instance, can inherit biases from their training data, resulting in unfair outcomes. To combat this, companies need to actively identify and mitigate these biases, promoting fairness and transparency. Embracing responsible innovation requires balancing technological advancements with ethical considerations, ensuring that technology benefits society while minimizing harm.

- *International Legal Issues:* Emerging technologies often transcend national borders, raising complex legal issues related to jurisdiction, cross-border data flows, and international cooperation. Harmonizing laws and regulations across different jurisdictions, promoting interoperability and standardization, and fostering international collaboration are essential for addressing these challenges. In essence, addressing the legal implications of emerging technologies is important for the society living inside a digital space. Cybercrimes should be given importance.

- *Skills Needed:* The profession of law has long been guarded with the assumption that legal knowledge and reasoning is a specialized skill that requires a highly educated and trained specialist to deliver. The legal service industry is witnessing a surge in specialization and niche expertise among paralegals. As the legal profession evolves, so do the skills required to succeed. Lawyers in the future will need more than just legal knowledge. Some of the essential skills that will define the future of law include technological competence and analytical thinking.

1.7 CONCLUSION

It is evident that emerging technologies are changing the legal field. New legal tech solutions, like AI-powered legal guidance and contract automation, are transforming the legal industry. Therefore, we must remain knowledgeable about these technologies and how they are applied to law practice as lawyers. Law and technology are no longer disconnected as technology for lawyers enhances the efficiency of legal services. However, technology, no matter how advanced, is not enough to create effective legal strategies. Law firms need to go beyond simply layering new technology onto old habits. They must rethink how they deliver value to clients, breaking free from the time-for-money mindset that limits innovation. They must be willing to rethink the traditional business model of a law firm.

The legal profession and the future law firm will be radically different as a result of the advancement of technology. The future of law is being shaped by several transformative trends. These trends are driving the evolution of legal practice and creating new opportunities for lawyers. The future of law is filled with opportunities for those willing to embrace change and adapt to emerging trends and technologies. While the future will need the law, it may not necessarily need lawyers to provide it. More information about emerging technologies in the law field can be found in the books [14-22] and a related journal: *Journal on Emerging Technologies.*

REFERENCE

[1] A. Dyranov and R. Chupryna, "The benefits of legal technology – How legal tech can improve your operations in 2025," March 2024.

https://spd.tech/legaltech-development/benefits-of-legal-technology/

[2] M. N. O. Sadiku, P. A. Adekunte, and J. O. Sadiku, "Emerging Technologies in the Law Field," *International Journal of Trend in Scientific Research and Development, vol. 9, no. 2*, March-April 2025, pp. 405-414.

[3] M. Halaweh, "Emerging technology: What is it?" *Journal of Technology Management & Innovation, vol. 8, no. 3*, 2013, pp. 108-115.

[4] N. Duggal, "Top 18 new technology trends for 2023," July 2023,

https://www.simplilearn.com/top-technology-trends-and-jobs-article

[5] "How enterprise architects integrate emerging technologies to enhance architecture,"

https://www.linkedin.com/pulse/how-enterprise-architects-integrate-emerging-technologies-qdgfe/

[6] C. Looney, "The future of paralegal support: emerging trends and technologies," July 2023,

https://www.ldmglobal.com/2023/07/06/paralegal-support-future/

[7] R. Kaushal, "How are emerging technologies reshaping the legal landscape?" May 2024.

https://www.legalsupportworld.com/blog/emerging-technologies-reshaping-the-legal-landscape/#:~:text=Emerging%20technologies%20are%20significantly%20reshaping,tasks%20such%20as%20advising%20clients.

[8] B. Arunda, "Impacts of emerging technologies on law and justice delivery," May 2, 2023, p. 102.

https://www.linkedin.com/pulse/impacts-emerging-technologies-law-justice-delivery-benjamin-arunda/

[9] A. Hamdan, "Top 10 legal tech trends of 2024," December 2024,

https://briefpoint.ai/legal-technology-trends/

[10] Legal Talk Network, "Emerging trends in legal tech," July 2, 2024, p. 108.

https://legaltalknetwork.com/blog/2024/07/emerging-trends-in-legal-tech/

[11] B. Majumdar, "Emerging technologies in law enforcement," June 2017,

https://exclusive.multibriefs.com/content/emerging-technologies-in-law-enforcement/law-enforcement-defense-security

[12] "Legal implications of emerging technologies," August 2024,

https://www.ceb.com/emerging-technologies-legal-corporate-compliance/

[13] "Legal implication of emerging technologies," March 2024.

https://www.linkedin.com/pulse/legal-implication-emerging-technologies-valscotech-eytdc/

[14] M. Vaid, *Law and Emerging Technologies*. University Publication, 2024.

[15] V. Sutton, *Emerging Technologies Law*. Vargas Publishing, 2015).

[16] L. Edwards, B. Schafer, and E. Harbinja (eds.), *Future Law: Emerging Technology, Regulation and Ethics*. Edinburgh University Press, 2020.

[17] R. D. Ryder and N. Naren, *Internet Law: Regulating Cyberspace and Emerging Technologies*. Bloomsbury Publishing

India Pvt. Ltd, 2020.

[18] T. Goldman, *Technology in the Law Office*. Pearson, 4th edition, 2014.

[19] E. T. Jensen, and R. T. P. Alcala (eds.), *The Impact of Emerging Technologies on the Law of Armed Conflict*. Oxford University Press, 2019.

[20] E. A. Morse, *Electronic Payment Systems: Law and Emerging Technologies*. American Bar Association, Business Law Section, 2018.

[21] G. E. Marchant, B. R. Allenby, and J. R. Herkert, *The Growing Gap Between Emerging Technologies and Legal-Ethical Oversight: The Pacing Problem*. Springer Netherlands, 2011.

[22] R. Raysman, *Emerging Technologies and the Law: Forms and Analysis – Volume 1*. Law Journal Press, 2002.

CHAPTER 2
ARTIFICIAL INTELLIGENCE IN LAW PRACTICE

"As computational technology and artificial intelligence matures, more people will be able to have better access to justice."

—Monica Bay

2.1 INTRODUCTION

Artificial Intelligence (AI) refers to the development of computer systems that can perform tasks that typically require human intelligence, such as learning, reasoning, perception, and decision-making. AI means the ability to acquire and apply knowledge through man made device. The goal of AI is to create intelligent machines that can perform tasks more efficiently, accurately, and autonomously than humans. AI is increasingly becoming a part of real, everyday life. It is progressively entering into the legal profession, changing the way in which lawyers carry out their work and provide their legal services to clients. AI is transforming the legal industry for lawyers, the courtroom, consumers, education, and the future of law practice. Today, the team human + AI is the winning formula, and this statement is fully applicable to the legal profession, where artificial intelligence is not a substitute for lawyers but a very powerful and indispensable complement to increase their effectiveness. Figure 2.1 shows AI symbol [1].

Figure 2.1 AI symbol [1].

Legal practice refers to works done primarily for the purpose of rendering legal advise or giving legal representation. The legal industry is experiencing a profound transformation driven by the rapid advancement of technology. Although the legal industry lags when it comes to embracing technology, AI is making its mark there too and there is no turning back. However, in the United States, courts seems more far ahead in technology adoption, as the US legal systems are heavily dependent on case law. From automating contract review and analysis to predicting litigation outcomes, AI is reshaping the legal landscape for the better. AI helps lawyers do their legal workload faster and saves them time [2].

Artificial intelligence (AI) refers to computer software and systems that do not just do tasks they have been programmed for in advance; they actually learn as they go, improving their performance through feedback. AI refers to inspiration of human intelligence processes by machines, particularly computer systems. AI has already begun to make its mark on various industries, and the legal profession is no exception. It is empowering legal professionals to exceed expectations, boost efficiency, enhance compliance, drive better decision-making, and improve client service [3].

This chapter discusses how and why corporate legal departments are embracing AI in their complex legal practice. It begins with discussing what artificial intelligence is all about. It describes generative AI. It discusses AI in legal practice and its applications.

It highlights the benefits and challenges of AI in legal practice. The last section concludes with comments.

2.2 WHAT IS ARTIFICIAL INTELLIGENCE?

The term "artificial intelligence" (AI) is an umbrella term John McCarthy, a computer scientist, coined in 1955 and de-fined as "the science and engineering of in-telligent machines." It refers to the ability of a computer system to perform human tasks (such as thinking and learning) that usually can only be accomplished using human intelligence [4]. Typically, AI systems demonstrate at least some of the following human behaviors: planning, learning, reasoning, problem solving, knowledge representation, perception, speech recognition, decision-making, language translation, motion, manipulation, intelligence, and creativity.

The 10 U.S. Code § 2358 define artificial intelligence as [5]:

1. "Any artificial system that performs tasks under varying and unpredictable circumstances without significant human oversight, or that can learn from experience and improve performance when exposed to data sets.

2. An artificial system developed in computer software, physical hardware, or other context that solves tasks requiring human-like perception, cognition, planning, learning, communication, or physical action.

3. An artificial system designed to think or act like a human, including cognitive architectures and neural networks.

4. A set of techniques, including machine learning, that is designed to approximate a cognitive task.

5. An artificial system designed to act rationally, including an intelligent software agent or embodied robot that achieves goals using perception, planning, reasoning, learning, communicating, decision making, and acting."

AI provides tools creating intelligent machines which can behave like humans, think like humans, and make decisions like humans. The main goals of artificial intelligence are [6]:

1. Replicate human intelligence

2. Solve knowledge-intensive tasks

3. Make an intelligent connection of perception and action

4. Build a machine which can perform tasks that requires human intelligence

5. Create some system which can exhibit intelligent behavior, learn new things by itself, demonstrate, explain, and can advise to its user.

AI is not a single technology but a range of computational models and algorithms. The concept of AI is an umbrella term that encompasses many different technologies. AI is not a single technology but a collection of techniques that enables computer systems to perform tasks that would otherwise require human intelligence. The major disciplines in AI include [7]:

- *Expert systems*

- *Fuzzy logic*

- *Neural networks*

- *Machine learning (ML)*

- *Deep learning*

- *Natural Language Processors (NLP)*

- *Robots*

These computer-based tools or technologies have been used to achieve AI's goals. Each AI tool has its own advantages. Using a combination of these models, rather than a single model, is recommended. Figure 2.2 shows a typical expert system, while Figure 2.3 illustrates the AI tools. These tools are gaining momentum across every industry. Analytics can be considered a core AI capability.

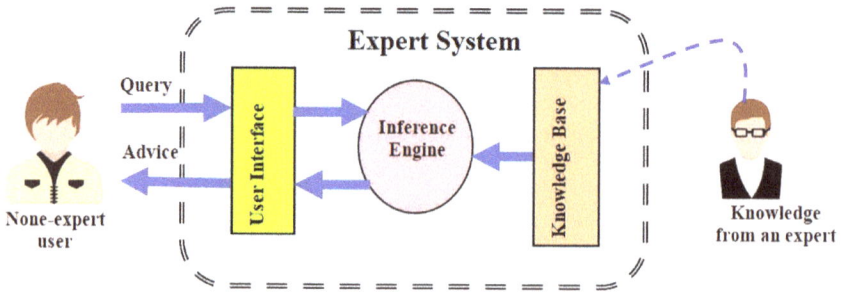

Figure 2.2 A typical expert system.

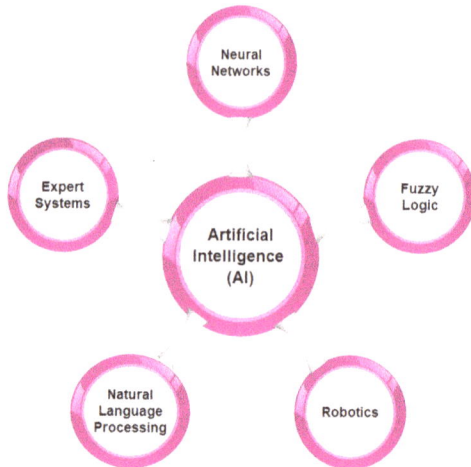

Figure 2.3 AI tools.

2.3 GENERATIVE AI

Artificial Intelligence (AI) is increasingly a part of our world and it is rapidly changing our lives. Generative AI (GenAI) is a subset of artificial intelligence that uses generative models to produce text, images, videos, or other forms of data. Generative AI (GenAI) is a term for any type of AI system capable of using generative models to create new forms of humanlike creative content, like text, images, music, audio, video and more. GenAI models include various algorithms able to learn the various patterns and structures of input training data before generating novel outputs with similar characteristics. It is essentially a narrow type and application of the broader artificial intelligence umbrella of technologies. It describes algorithms (such as ChatGPT) that can be used to create new content, including audio, code, images, text, simulations, and videos. It is specifically designed and trained to generate new content. The versatility and potential of GenAI to transform various aspects of business operations make it an attractive investment for companies across industries. GenAI uses neural networks, machine learning, deep learning models, complex algorithms, and large and varied training datasets to produce original content based on user input and how to reason in ways akin to a human brain. The technology is built on AI tools shown in Figure 2.4 [8]. It uses neural networks to identify the patterns and structures within existing data to generate new and original content.

Defining Generative AI

To understand generative artificial intelligence (GenAI), we first need to understand how the technology builds from each of the AI subcategories listed below.

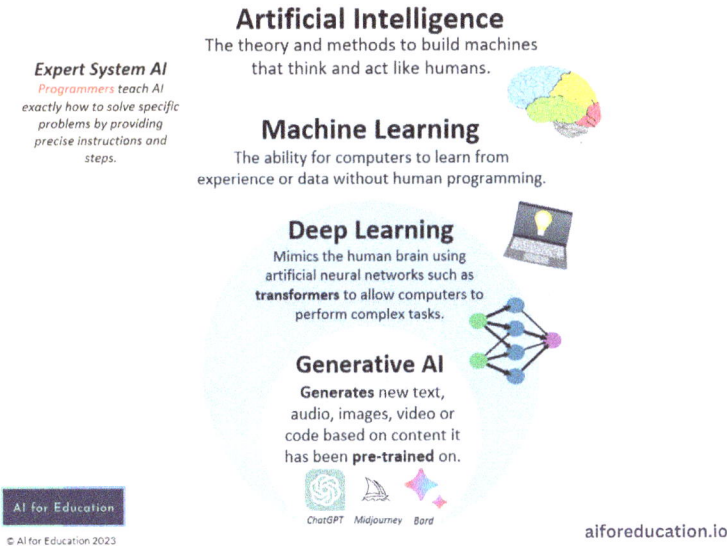

Artificial Intelligence
The theory and methods to build machines that think and act like humans.

Expert System AI
Programmers teach AI exactly how to solve specific problems by providing precise instructions and steps.

Machine Learning
The ability for computers to learn from experience or data without human programming.

Deep Learning
Mimics the human brain using artificial neural networks such as **transformers** to allow computers to perform complex tasks.

Generative AI
Generates new text, audio, images, video or code based on content it has been **pre-trained** on.

ChatGPT   Midjourney   Bard

AI for Education
© AI for Education 2023

aiforeducation.io

Figure 2.4 GenAI built on AI tools listed above [8].

Generative AI can be thought of as a machine-learning model that is trained to create new data, rather than making a prediction about a specific dataset. Since its inception, the field of machine learning used both discriminative models and generative models, to model and predict data. A generative AI system is constructed by applying unsupervised machine learning or self-supervised machine learning to a data set. The most common way to train a generative AI model is to use supervised learning. Generative AI can also be trained on the motions of a robotic system to generate new trajectories for motion planning or navigation. Generative AI models are used to power chatbot products such as ChatGPT [9].

GenAI has the potential to change — in some cases radically — how legal professionals do their jobs in the years to come. Law firms using GenAI systems are already posting greater efficiencies in legal research and document management. AI (GenAI) assistants will become indispensable to practically every lawyer. Many professionals including those working in court systems may think of GenAI as public-facing tools like ChatGPT.

2.4 AI IN LEGAL PRACTICE

Over the past few years, legal professionals have become less wary of artificial intelligence. Figure 2.5 shows some legal professionals [10]. They are increasingly embracing AI as a transformative force, becoming more and more optimistic about the positive impact it can have on legal practices. Imagine a world where legal professionals can sift through mountains of case law in seconds, predict the outcomes of trials with remarkable accuracy, and automate tedious contract reviews—all thanks to artificial intelligence.

Figure 2.5 Some legal professionals [10].

The legal industry is undergoing a profound transformation driven by advancements in technology, particularly with the rise of artificial lawyers—AI-powered systems that perform tasks traditionally handled by human lawyers. In recent years, related technological advances have allowed legal teams to automate or expedite work that has traditionally been done by entry-level colleagues. Today, some lawyers use AI to automate routine tasks such as contract review, research, and generative legal writing. Figure 2.6 represents legal practice [11], while Figure 2.7 represents AI in legal practice [12].

Figure 2.6 Representation of the legal practice [11].

Figure 2.7 Representation of AI in legal practice [12].

Legal work, well known for its long hours and heavy workloads, is being revolutionized by artificial intelligence, specifically generative AI. Artificial intelligence improves the efficiency of legal work by way of automation. From streamlining legal research and enhancing contract management to employing predictive analytics and revolutionizing e-discovery, AI tools are reshaping how law firms operate, making processes faster, more accurate, and highly efficient. AI tools can now handle the endless reading, summarizing, creating, and filing of documents ordinarily relegated to junior attorneys or paralegals. The tools are already being leveraged in several legal practices, including [13]:

- Due Diligence
- Prediction Analytics
- Contract Analysis
- Contract Review
- Legal Document Generation
- e-discovery
- Legal Research
- Contract Negotiation
- Document management
- Deep analytics insights
- Customer service
- Language analytics
- Dispute resolution

2.5 APPLICATIONS OF AI IN LEGAL PRACTICE

AI has been successfully applied in various sectors such as education, healthcare, finance, manufacturing, and transportation, where it has make significant improvements in efficiency, cost reduction, and the development of innovative products and services. The technology can be used to assist in legal research, perform contract analysis, and even generate contracts, agreement, and other legal documents. The primary areas where AI is being applied in the law include review of documents, legal research, legal education, contract and legal document analysis, proofreading, document generation, and more. Some of these areas are covered here [14-16]:

• *Intellectual Property:* This encompasses a broad spectrum of intangible assets, including patents, copyrights, trademarks, and trade secrets. AI has become a game changer across various sectors, and intellectual property (IP) law is no exception. The convergence of IP and AI presents both unparalleled opportunities and unique challenges for businesses across industries. The legal challenges the new technology presents are formidable, particularly at the intersection of AI and intellectual property. The use of proprietary material in training AI systems and the potential exposure of confidential information pose significant risks.

• *Copyright:* Copyright law protects original works of authorship, such as literary, artistic, and musical works. Copyrights are a form of intellectual property protected by federal law. Owning a copyright gives the owner the exclusive right to reproduce, publish, or sell an original work of authorship, such as a book, a painting, or a song. Although copyright law does not specifically address artificial intelligence, protection under the Copyright Act must meet the following requirements: (1) an original work of authorship; (2) fixed in a tangible medium; (3) that has a minimal amount of creativity. Any work that does not meet the three requirements does not qualify for copyright protection. Since machine-created work may not need the criteria for copyright protection, ownership may not be clearly distinguished. A lawyer advising an AI company will need to develop new law and provide recommendations about how the law will be applied to issues of copyright infringement.

• *AI-generated Art:* Artists using traditional mediums, such as paint, pen, or paper, are considered the authors of the work and generally hold copyright over their work by default. The fundamental question before addressing AI-created art is whether copyright can belong to anyone other than a human being. Figure 2.8 shows a typical AI-generated art [17].

Figure 2.8 AI-generated art [17].

It is safe to state that artificial intelligence generated art is here to stay. So once an AI-generated masterpiece is created, what stops someone from claiming it as their own and using it commercially or preventing others from using it? On top of existentially threatening the very concept of artists and creatives, AI-generated content raises several new legal issues. Ultimately humans are the ones that make the final decision to use art generated by a machine and AI clearly cannot grant permission for use of the work or hold a copyright.

• *Patent:* A patent grants its owner the exclusive right to exclude others from making, using, selling, and importing an invention for a limited period, usually 20 years from the filing date. The patent world is discussing whether an AI can be listed as an "inventor" on a patent application. It is not beyond imagination that Artificial General Intelligence may find its way as a "legal person" or may have laws specifically drafted for its regulation and ownership in the near future.

• *Trade Secrets:* These encompass confidential information that provides a competitive advantage to its owner. AI technologies, such as machine learning models, training data, and algorithms, may be considered trade secrets if they meet the necessary requirements of confidentiality, economic value, and reasonable efforts to maintain secrecy.

• Contracts: Contracts serve as the backbone of our economic structure; they are indispensable for any business transaction. However, the whole procedure of mediating and yet the process of negotiating and settling a contract is a hassle. Administering the signing of the contract, overseeing and supervising it can prove to be a pain. The lawyers from both parties are required to manually inspect, refine, and swap red-lined documents in a repetitive manner. This whole process provides huge potential for automation. AI-based solutions are helping legal teams offload the mundane aspects of reviewing and redlining contracts so that they can focus on more high-impact work. AI can be used to automate the drafting and review of contracts, as well as to identify potential issues and inconsistencies. ChatGPT can assist in writing legal documents such as contracts and it is also used for legal translation.

• *Chatbots:* AI-powered chatbots are already streamlining the intake and triage of legal requests. Bots can prove to be highly effective in offering legal help and in providing the masses with easy access to services. A lawyer bot is basically software that has the capacity of carrying out automated tasks which generally get performed by lawyers. These bots are useful for boosting the speed of the work and in offering an enhanced experience by enabling the clients to self-serve themselves online.

• *Due Diligence:* Uncovering background information through the due diligence process is another time-consuming process that legal practitioners spend their time on. The AI-powered platforms can assist in accelerating the process and in cutting down time. Acceleration of the due diligence process would have a considerable impact since it would aid in verifying current figures as well as facts from the prior cases. The due diligence procedure is generally a hassle for humans and AI would play a massive role in boosting the accuracy. AI-powered tools can quickly analyze and categorize large volumes of documents, which can be especially helpful in the discovery phase of litigation and during due diligence processes. Legal professionals who wish to perform due diligence on the use of AI in their practices need to do so thoughtfully and rigorously.

• *Legal Document Review:* Legal document review is a tedious and time-consuming task, but AI systems have revolutionized this process. Generative AI systems, utilizing natural language processing, are now capable of understanding and responding to plain English questions. Using AI for document review can significantly reduce the time and effort required to determine document relevance and legal privilege. It guarantees that all documents undergo thorough review and comply with pertinent regulations. Figure 2.9 represents AI in legal document review [18].

Figure 2.9 Representation of AI in legal document review [18].

• *Predictive Analytics:* Predictive analytics is transforming strategic planning in the legal industry. By analyzing historical legal data, case precedents, and other relevant factors, machine learning models can forecast litigation outcomes and inform strategic decisions. Predictive analytics can also aid in filing motions by analyzing historical data from similar cases, court rulings, and judge-specific trends to forecast the likelihood of a motion being granted or denied. Figure 2.10 shows a typical court setting [18].

Figure 2.10 A typical court setting [18].

• *Legal Research:* Legal research is one of the most important aspects of the legal practice. Before the advent of artificial intelligence, lawyers have to spend days or hours researching cases and flipping through the volumes of books when making legal research. AI systems have the capacity to search and analyze vast amounts of legal information in a fraction of the time it takes a human. As these tools become more accurate and efficient, traditional legal research roles may be replaced by AI-driven solutions. As law schools try to meet the demands of a booming industry, the focus on applied research in AI and emerging technologies is also expanding.

• *Legal Education:* AI is making its mark on legal education. Many law schools and professors are proactively incorporating AI into the classroom. Law school curriculums will need to keep pace with changes in technology law, ethics, and data science. Law schools are integrating AI into their curricula, offering courses on AI ethics, data science, and technology law. These curriculum changes ensure that future lawyers are equipped with the skills needed to navigate the evolving legal landscape. Law schools are also updating their academic integrity policies to address the influence of generative AI.

2.6 BENEFITS

Lawyers play a critical role in upholding the rule of law and maintaining a just society. Artificial intelligence plays a very significant role in the modern legal practice. AI empowers lawyers to do their job better, faster, and smarter. Advances in AI will change the nature of legal work for lawyers, helping to make them more effective and efficient.

Artificial intelligence for lawyers automates routine tasks, enhances efficiency, and minimizes errors. Along with overtaking paperwork and handling of data, it is also aiding the industry towards becoming more consumer-centric. Other benefits of AI in law include [12,13]:

• *AI Saves Time:* The biggest, most obvious benefit to AI applications is time savings. Computer systems can analyze more information, more thoroughly than humans can, in a tiny fraction of the time. This benefit applies to all types of AI applications. Computers can quickly search through and identify discoverable or potentially relevant data of all forms and file types. Obviously, those time savings can translate into monetary savings, since less attorney or staff time is involved in finding answers and identifying mistakes.

• *Automation:* Automation refers to technologies that use rules to carry out tasks. AI is changing the way legal services are provided by automating repetitive tasks, streamlining document management and location, processing a tremendous amount of information and refining contract review. AI technology in the legal field automates many of the repetitive duties that keep attorneys at the office until late in the night, creating all-too-common burnout.

• *Streamlining Legal Processes:* We all know that a lawyer's time is valuable…and expensive. Finding ways to save time in the legal industry, yet remain accurate and compliant, is critical. Law practices can be streamlined through automation and introduce an AI solution to help. AI will assist with and accelerate critical parts of legal services, including comprehensive document review, exhausting proofreading and rigorous legal research.

• *Quality Assurance in Legal Documentation:* Leveraging AI for quality assurance and legal reviews is becoming more and more necessary as it meticulously reads and summarizes relevant documents and then discloses any discrepancies or inaccurate data findings. It will locate specific clauses, potential risks or obligations associated with the company instantly, saving time, effort, and energy.

• *Strategic Decision-Making:* Human judgment and human expertise will always be necessary in the area of legal practices. No matter how smart machine learning, AI algorithms, and AI tools are, the legal profession still relies on humans to uphold ethical standards, share valuable insights and perform strategic work. Using similar case law and having concrete data that highlights those outcomes, legal professionals can form new strategies or change existing strategies that will likely yield positive conclusions

• *Reducing Workload and Stress:* AI not only alleviates redundant, time-consuming in-house staff workload, it ultimately plays a role in creating higher job satisfaction, reducing attorney stress, and minimizing work frustration. By allowing AI to perform administrative tasks and offer support in drafting, document analysis, and more, a legal professional can focus their time on higher-value, strategic duties that utilize their trained legal expertise.

• *Enhancing In-House Client Service:* When legal professionals are forced to focus their time staring at endless documents and data, client phone calls go unanswered, emails get ignored, and clients are left feeling unimportant. AI enables in-house lawyers to focus more on strategic legal advising and less on mundane tasks, which improve service for internal and external clients. Less time spent on low-level, monotonous responsibilities means attorneys have time and opportunity to engage more in human-specific activities. AI also equips legal teams with better information and legal research, helping build better cases, yielding positive results, and ultimately makes their clients happy.

• *Reducing Litigation Costs:* Proponents of legal AI have

pointed out that the technology has the potential to provide greater access to justice for litigants with limited resources. Because machine learning can help lawyers speed up the due diligence process by analyzing cases more efficiently, this decreases the risk that litigation funders need to take.

• *Increased Efficiency:* AI is quickly becoming a necessary tool to stay competitive in today's legal industry, especially when it comes to legal research, one of the most time-consuming tasks that legal professionals are forced to do with nearly every case. AI assists lawyers by finding the authoritative sources and can even rank them by relevance. It can extract key information, provide a summary of each document, or compare the documents according to specified data. Artificial lawyers can handle repetitive tasks such as document review, legal research, and contract analysis more quickly and accurately than humans. They can also operate round the clock without breaks, providing continuous support, and reducing turnaround times.

• *Cost Reduction:* Firms can save on labor costs by employing robot lawyers for tasks that would otherwise require human paralegals or junior associates. Reduced costs can make legal services more accessible to individuals and small businesses who might not afford traditional legal assistance.

2.7 CHALLENGES

Unfortunately, AI can also negatively impact the legal field. For example, AI's ability to create deep fake technology can spread harmful misinformation and disinformation. This is especially a concern for lawyers who work in intellectual property law. AI is not going to complete the whole process of filing a statement of claim without human input and checks. Lawyers must navigate issues such as algorithmic bias, hallucinations, and confidentiality concerns when using AI in their practice. The use of AI in legal practice raises unprecedented legal questions that require new rules and thoughtful navigation. Other challenges of AI in law practice include the following [12,19]:

• *Data Privacy:* With AI tools processing sensitive legal documents, data security and compliance are paramount. Clients demand confidentiality, and breaches can lead to severe repercussions. It is important to have robust cybersecurity measures that ensure AI applications align with ethical and regulatory standards.

• *Ethical Concern:* Many legal professionals have reported being concerned that GenAI usage could put them or their firms in violation of ethical and professional codes of conduct. Currently, there are no clear industry-wide and fully-agreed-upon guidelines as to how to proceed. What lawyers have to do at present is monitor developments from the state to international level to get a sense of how ethical codes of conduct are evolving in the AI era. It may come down to each law firm creating its own ethical playbook for using GenAI.

• *Risks:* The use of AI in handling sensitive legal information increases the risk of data breaches and cyberattacks. Ensuring the confidentiality of client information managed by artificial lawyers is critical and can be challenging. Using AI-based models carry a substantial degree of risk. The main risks identified are taking away jobs, vulnerable to cyber-attacks, economic constraints, untrained lawyers, IP rights, privacy and data protection and ethical issues. While it is important to move forward, it is no less important to do so in a safe, ethical, and sustainable way. Lawyers are required to protect all client information from both intentional and inadvertent disclosure. A key ethical duty that lawyers have is ensuring that the use of AI solutions does not pose a risk to their duty to preserve client confidentiality and to maintain the attorney-client privilege.

• *Skills Gap:* Adopting AI requires tech-savvy lawyers, yet not all professionals possess the necessary skills. This "skills gap" challenges firms seeking seamless AI adoption. Training programs are essential to bridge this digital divide, ensuring lawyers are equipped to work alongside AI tools.

• *Job Replacement:* As AI disrupts the legal profession, it raises questions about who, or what, can be a lawyer. Maybe AI will not replace all lawyers outright. But it can still provide sound legal advice. Anybody, any entity, can provide legal information, including AI systems. As artificial intelligence approaches the bar, human lawyers will not be sent back to the bench just yet. AI does not understand that nuance, and could draw conclusions that may not produce the best result for a client. There are still many aspects of the legal profession that no amount of AI development would likely be able to automate or replace. The future of lawyering is not about the wholesale replacement of lawyers by AI. Instead, it is about the emergence of a symbiotic relationship, where AI augments human capabilities, empowers more informed decision-making, and frees lawyers to focus on the higher-order aspects of legal practice. The automation of routine tasks may lead to fewer job opportunities for paralegals and junior lawyers.

• *Regulations:* For centuries, regulations of the legal profession have made it clear there cannot be an engagement in legal practice by unqualified entities. In other words, the practice of law is limited to those admitted as licensed legal practitioners in the jurisdiction. AI does not have to comply with ethical responsibilities like a duty to act in the client's best interest that sets lawyers apart.

2.8 CONCLUSION

Artificial intelligence (AI) has been paving its way towards emerging as the backbone factor in the legal profession. The changes brought by the use of AI tools impact the foundational principles of the duties governing the legal profession, and the rights of clients and citizens. There is clearly great promise in what AI tools can and will do to support legal professionals in their work. Although AI technology still remains in the initial stage, it has the potential of unleashing significant opportunities to revolutionize and rejuvenate the law industry in the near future. Empowered by technology, lawyers are more productive, allowing more legal matters to be represented around the world.

It is evident that AI is impacting the legal profession, and this technology is here to stay. AI will create new opportunities for the legal profession. The future of legal practice has never looked brighter. Some law schools are increasingly incorporating AI into their curriculums in order to prepare lawyers for using AI in their practices and advising clients on AI-related matters. More information on artificial intelligence in law practice industry is available from the books in [20-25] and the following related journals.

- *The AI Journal*
- *AI Magazine*
- *Energy and AI*
- *Journal of Intelligence*
- *Artificial Intelligence and Law*
- *Journal of Digital Technologies and Law*

REFERENCE

[1] "The rise of artificial intelligence in construction industry," June 2022,

https://gharpedia.com/blog/artificial-intelligence-in-construction/

[2] D. Thakore, "How artificial intelligence (AI) revolutionizes legal practice — it is the future of law," July 2023.

https://medium.com/the-generator/how-artificial-intelligence-ai-revolutionizes-legal-practice-it-is-the-future-of-law-e628eac11775

[3] M. N. O. Sadiku, S. A. Ajayi, and J. O. Sadiku, "Artificial intelligence in legal practice: Opportunities, challenges, and future directions," *Journal of Engineering Research and Reports, vol. 27, no. 4*, pp. 68-80.

[4] M. N. O. Sadiku, "Artificial intelligence," IEEE Potentials, May 1989, pp. 35-39.

[5] "Artificial intelligence (AI),"

https://www.law.cornell.edu/wex/artificial_intelligence_(ai)

[6] "Artificial intelligence tutorial,"

https://www.javatpoint.com/artificial-intelligence-tutorial

[7] D. Quinby, "Artificial intelligence and the future of travel," May 2017,

https://www.phocuswright.com/Travel-Research/Research-Updates/2017/Artificial-Intelligence-and-the-Future-of-Travel

[8] "Generative AI explainer," Unknown Source.

[9] M. N. O. Sadiku, P. A. Adekunte, and J. O. Sadiku, "Generative artificial intelligence," *International Journal of Trend in Scientific Research and Development, vol. 8, no. 6*, November-December 2024, pp. 561-570.

[10] "The role of AI in modern legal practice," August 2024.

https://copymate.app/blog/the-role-of-ai-in-modern-legal-practice/

[11] D. Faggella, "AI in law and legal practice – A comprehensive view of 35 current applications," September 2021.

https://emerj.com/ai-in-law-legal-practice-current-applications/

[12] "Artificial lawyers: The future of legal practice or just a myth?" July 2024.

https://www.runsensible.com/blog/artificial-lawyers-legal-practice/

[13] J. Levine, " 7 Benefits of AI in the legal industry," May 2024,

https://contractpodai.com/news/ai-benefits-legal/

[14] M. N. O. Sadiku, P. O. Adebo, and J. O. Sadiku, "Artificial intelligence law: An overview," *International Journal of Trend in Research and Development*, vol. 13, no. 3, May-June 2024, pp. 38-42.

[15] A. Mathur, "Art-istic or art-ificial? Ownership and copyright concerns in AI-generated artwork," November

https://itsartlaw.org/2022/11/21/artistic-or-artificial-ai/

[16] G. Mukundan, "Intersection of artificial intelligence and intellectual property laws," April 2023,

https://acuraip.com/the-intersection-of-artificial-intelligence-and-intellectual-property-law/

[17] https://writesonic.com/photosonic-ai-art-generator

[18] A. Olsen, "Transforming legal practice: How artificial intelligence for lawyers is changing the field," August 2024.

https://iplawusa.com/transforming-legal-practice-how-artificial-intelligence-for-lawyers-is-changing-the-field/#:~:text=Artificial%20intelligence%20is%20revolutionizing%20the,tasks%20more%20swiftly%20and%20accurately.

[19] "AI in legal practice: Balancing efficiency and employment," December 10, 2024.

https://quantilus.com/article/ai-in-legal-practice-balancing-efficiency-and-employment/

[20] M. N. O. Sadiku, S. M. Musa, and S. R. Nelatury, *Applications of Artificial Intelligence*. Sherida, NY: Gotham Books, 2022.

[21] M. N. O. Sadiku, *Law in the Digital Age*. Las Vegas, NV: Book Films Media, 2024.

[22] K. D. Ashley, *Artificial Intelligence and Legal Analytics: New Tools for Law Practice in the Digital Age*. Cambridge University Press, 2017.

[23] H. Arora, *Artificial Intelligence in Law Enforcement: Use-Cases, Impact on Fundamental Rights and Ethical Reflections*. Eliva Press, 2023.

[24] N. Waisberg and A. Hudek, *AI For Lawyers: How Artificial Intelligence is Adding Value, Amplifying Expertise, and Transforming Careers*. Wiley, 2021.

[25] B. Custers and E. Fosch-Villaronga (eds.), *Law and Artificial Intelligence: Regulating AI and Applying AI in Legal Practice (Information Technology and Law Series, 35)*. T.M.C. Asser Press, 2022.

CHAPTER 3
LEGAL AUTOMATION

"It is change, continuing change, inevitable change, that is the dominant factor in society today. No sensible decision can be made any longer without taking into account not only the world as it is, but the world as it will be.... This, in turn, means that our statesmen, our businessmen, our everyman must take on a science fictional way of thinking."

—Isaac Asimov

3.1 INTRODUCTION

By nature, legal work is a mixture of high-level advisory work and routine tasks. Legal work has always been document-heavy, detail-oriented, and time-sensitive, as evident by a pile of documents shown in Figure 3.1 [1].

Figure 3.1 Legal work traditionally involves a pile of documents [1].

Many legal professionals find themselves bogged down by repetitive tasks that could be handled more efficiently with technology. Corporate legal departments are constantly faced with the challenge to do more with less. All areas of legal practice that include repeatable, standardizable work product can be automated. These areas can be automated to levels far beyond the industry's current level of adoption of legal technology for practice management.

Legal automation simplifies time-consuming tasks, giving lawyers more time to focus on higher-value work. The automation of legal work is a win for law firm owners, legal associates, and paralegals as well. Automation enables legal teams to meet unrelenting client demands to do "more for less and faster-better-cheaper" [2]. It brings major changes to the legal sector, affecting more than 60% of daily tasks. Figure 3.2 shows a representation of automation [3].

Figure 3.2 A representation of automation [3].

Automation involves the creation of computer software and automated systems that can complete repeatable processes and reduce the need for human intervention. Over the past decade, automation has dramatically changed how companies do business. Automation is transforming the law profession. Legal automation involves the application of software to automate the manual or routine tasks traditionally performed by legal professionals. Automation simplifies repetitive tasks, freeing up time and resources for more strategic work. Whether it is drafting contracts or generating compliance documents, automation allows teams to work faster and more accurately [4].

In this chapter, we will examine how automation is being applied in different legal practice areas. The chapter begins with explaining what legal automation is. It discusses different types of legal automation. It covers the applications of legal automation. It highlights the benefits and challenges of legal automation. The last section concludes with comments.

3.2 WHAT IS LEGAL AUTOMATION?

The legal industry has long been marked by tradition, libraries full of case law, complex contracts scrutinized line by line, and endless administrative work. For years, lawyers have relied on paper to handle their immense workload of correspondence and legal documents. Lawyers spend an enormous amount of time doing paperwork. Routine tasks of lawyers involve redundant, time-consuming, and tedious paperwork. The right combination of skilled employees and automation can save a lot of paperwork. Automation of legal paperwork processing enhances the operations of an organization. Figure 3.3 shows how lawyers need to do less with paper [2]. Traditional legal processes, from contract management to compliance tracking, often need to be faster and more error-prone. These inefficiencies lead to delayed operations and increase the risk of non-compliance. Legal automation offers a powerful solution.

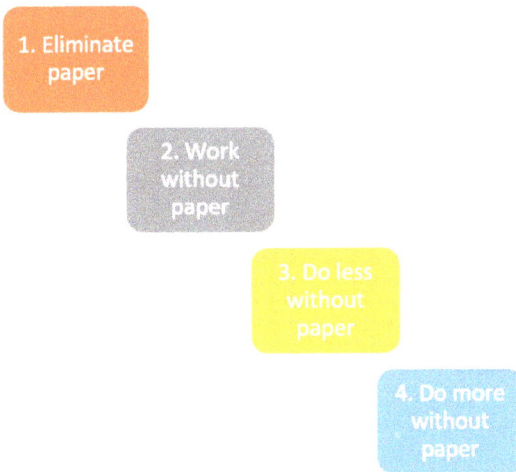

Figure 3.3 How lawyers need to do less with paper [2].

Legal automation refers to the application of technology to perform tasks traditionally handled by legal professionals. It involves using software that is specifically designed to progress, manage and complete repeatable tasks/workflows or processes which are necessary for the delivery of legal services. The software enables legal teams to streamline processes like document creation, contract management, compliance tracking, and case management, allowing legal teams to focus on complex decision-making instead of routine administrative work.

Legal automation is best deployed to automate all the low-value, low-risk legal work so that lawyers can focus on the high-value, high-risk work. The best place to begin the implementation of legal technology is with mundane, repetitive tasks that consume time better spent doing more valuable things. The best kind of tasks to automate are ones you do regularly. Focus on finding tasks that take a long time, or things that are done the same way every time. Not everything can or should be automated. Processes need to be predictable for automation to work. Unique documents or anything that requires individual consultation, decision-making, or collaboration are not good candidates for automation. There are some common elements of legal workflows that lend themselves to automation quite naturally. Some examples include [5].

1. Contract drafting

2. Contract review

3. Document filing

4. Legal research

5. Legal compliance

6. Due diligence

7. IP protection

8. Document retrieval

9. Document creation

3.3 TYPES OF LEGAL AUTOMATION

Since lots of legal tasks can be automated, various technologies can be used for legal automation, from AI assistants through to eDiscovery and document management tools. There are plenty of opportunities to automate legal processes, and different tools will enable you to automate different tasks. This leads to the following types of legal automation [6]:

- *AI legal assistants:* AI-powered tools automate research, document review, and basic inquiries, reducing time spent on repetitive tasks. These usually take the form of an AI chatbot, like ChatGPT for lawyers.

- *Contract review and analysis:* AI-driven contract tools speed up review processes, identifying risks and inconsistencies with greater accuracy.

- *Automated workflows:* No-code automation platforms streamline manual tasks, improving processes like inquiry handling and case triage.

- *Risk and compliance management:* Automated tools help track regulatory changes and flag potential compliance risks.

- *Knowledge management:* AI-powered research tools compile and deliver relevant legal knowledge to teams efficiently.

- *Obligation management:* Automated contract renewal reminders and obligation tracking ensure deadlines are met. Functionality like automated contract renewal reminders can be used to automate obligation management work.

By automating these areas, legal professionals can dedicate more time to strategy, client relationships, and higher-value work. Each type of legal automation serves a distinct purpose.

3.4 APPLICATIONS OF LEGAL AUTOMATION

Many law firms are now automating document processing due to speed, accuracy, consistency, savings, and customer satisfaction. Automation is fast becoming the only way to keep up with the advancing speed of business. It is not just about doing work faster, it is also about doing it better. Specific applications of legal automation include the following [1,6]:

• *Legal Operations:* Disciplines like legal operations have emerged and are seeing legal departments run like a business and focus on optimizing the delivery of legal services to their business clients. Legal automation is a key pillar of any legal operations. While other legal technology may help lawyers organize and manage their work, legal automation uniquely shifts the type of work of legal departments to enable them to truly do more with less. Figure 3.4 shows a group of lawyers at work [7].

Figure 3.4 A group of lawyers at work [7].

• *Document Automation:* Drafting documents has fallen further down on the priority list amid growing demands and tightening resources. Law firms are currently pursuing strategies to increase operational efficiency as well as a reduction of operating costs to meet clients' growing expectations. Automation of legal documents is the force that lets law firms optimize their working processes, decrease the rate of mistakes, and maintain the competition. Legal document automation helps firms create, review, and manage documents with minimal manual input. In fact, legal automation tools can help law firms save up to 40% of their time by automating repetitive tasks. This efficiency allows legal teams to focus on high-impact work instead of manually drafting every document from scratch. With automation software, firms can save time and eliminate the possibility of making mistakes when it comes to preparing contracts, compliance forms, and agreements. Automating the creation of standard documents means less time spent on manual entry so that lawyers can focus on client interactions or case strategy. Legal document automation opens the path to efficiency, accuracy, and greater client satisfaction. Figure 3.5 represents document automation [8], while Figure 3.6 presents how it works [9].

Figure 3.5 Representation of document automation [8].

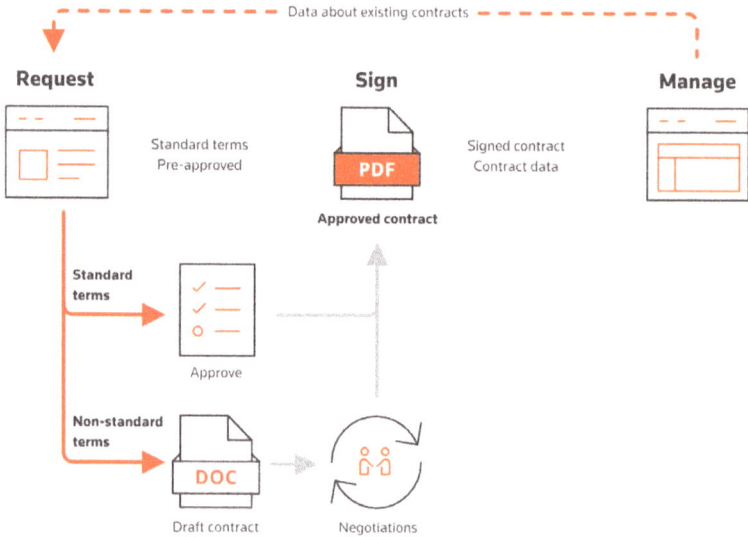

Figure 3.6 How legal document automation process works [9].

• *Contract Automation:* Legal document automation applies to different contracts, and contract generation is one of the most popular automation types. Contracts, specifically smart contracts, are another area with a lot of new investment in automation. Smart contracts use blockchain technology to execute agreements automatically when predefined conditions are met. This reduces the need for intermediaries, ensures contract security, and improves efficiency in contract execution. Reviewing contracts and conducting legal research are some of the most time-consuming aspects of legal work. AI-powered contract review tools scan documents for risks, inconsistencies, and missing clauses. With automation, firms can reduce the risk of oversight and handle cases more efficiently.

• *Workflow Automation:* Legal workflow automation helps law firms automate routine tasks. It streamlines processes like contract approvals, case tracking, and compliance monitoring. Instead of manually tracking progress, automation tools notify relevant team members about pending tasks, reducing bottlenecks and improving overall efficiency. With legal workflow automation, law firms can automate anything from billing to document management while reducing errors and decreasing overhead. Legal workflow automation technology provides limitless opportunities when it comes to helping you save time on key law firm processes, like client intake, document automation, client communications, payment collections, client reviews, and more. It gives your law firm the advantage of servicing clients and attracting new business more efficiently.

• *Compliance Documentation:* Compliance is a critical topic for law firms, and document automation enables organizations to keep up to date with new and changing rules. The firm will only require occasional manual tweaking of the document in a few compliance areas and record keeping.

• *Employment Agreements:* Employment law agreement drafting and implementation demands expediency. An automated system is convenient for issuing employment contracts by applying pre-set templates, introducing uniformity into document issuance, and reducing administrative delay.

• *eSignature:* An eSignature (or electronic signature) is a means by which a person can indicate their agreement with the content of a document or set of data. Like its handwritten counterpart in the offline world, an electronic signature is a legal concept capturing the signatory's intent to be bound by the terms of the signed document. In the age of new technologies, esignatures are among the tools that a legal professional cannot do without. E-signing allows clients and colleagues to sign papers electronically, which is far more effective and safer than paper. Figure 3.7 shows an example of signature [8].

Figure 3.7 An example of signature [8].

• *Document Assembly:* One popular automation in legal services is document assembly. By identifying frequently used legal documents, such as fee agreements and contracts, you can set up document templates in the software. Save your templates in the software and select them as needed. Templates can include additional prompts, like entering a fee for billing or setting a calendar appointment with a client.

• *Chatbots:* One significant advancement of AI technology has been the development of chatbots, such as ChatGPT models. These language models have the capacity to understand and generate human-like text responses, which can be helpful for lawyers as they work on various legal tasks. AI models such as ChatGPT and others have been employed to automate and enhance legal processes. Bots can receive and send emails, collect data from forms or scanned documents, log into applications, prepare reports, and much more. They are the perfect solution for organizations in which employees waste time on boring work.

• *Robotic Process Automation:* RPA ensures less risky and consistent work with trustworthy data. It involves the creation of software robots which complete simple tasks in the same way employees would, only much faster. This technology allows a legal team to focus on the difficult problems and human contact with clients, which improves their capacity and the quality of their service. RPA can help in processing data from various documents. For example, a bot can read a scanned contract and extract the parties' data. A well-constructed RPA solution allows you to use encryption and other technological solutions that ensure security. The zero-touch environment of robotic process automation helps to mitigate human-related risks in legal operations. An automated environment is free from biases, prejudices or variability, all of which mar human work with the risk of error.

• *Legal Research Assistance:* Legal research has historically been one of the most time-consuming tasks for lawyers. AI tools are now streamlining this process by offering real-time, context-aware search capabilities that go beyond mere keyword matching.

3.5 BENEFITS

Through legal automation, teams are empowered to create self-serve and self-help tools for their clients. Automation creates a happier workplace through streamlined processes, reduced mistakes and risk, elimination of tedious tasks, improved communication, better teamwork between law firm staff, staff undertaking higher value, and more. The main benefit of legal automation is an increase in productivity and significant time saving. This can have several obvious benefits, depending on what the lawyers in question choose to do with the time they gain back. Other benefits of legal automation include the following [10]:

• *Improved Accuracy:* Automation eliminates human error, so the documents are uniform and always up to code; with high level of accuracy. It is possible to build trust with clients while protecting a firm from potential fallout in a courtroom.

• *Cost Savings:* Cost savings are another big plus, with automation helping to cut down on time and resources spent on administrative tasks. By automating document workflows, law firms reduce overhead costs linked to manual labor and extensive document review processes. The time saved through automation translates into reduced staffing needs for administrative work and a more cost-effective practice.

• *Time Savings:* In the fast-paced legal industry, time is not just money; it is the backbone of efficiency and client satisfaction. Automation also frees up lawyers' time to focus on higher-value work, which can improve client satisfaction as firms can respond more swiftly to client needs. It gives time back to legal teams and help them refocus on high impact tasks by creating automation and self-service journeys for the low complexity tasks. Reducing time on routine tasks for engagements and strategy would give firms more resources to take an edge in this market. Figure 3.8 shows the significance of time savings [11].

	WITHOUT DOCUMENT AUTOMATION	WITH DOCUMENT AUTOMATION
Lease	60 Minutes	24 Minutes
License for Alterations	30 Minutes	12 Minutes
Rent Deposit Deed	18 Minutes	6 Minutes
Total	1 Hour 48 Minutes	42 Minutes

Figure 3.8 Significance of time savings [11].

• *Improved Efficiency:* This process eliminates the need for lawyers to spend valuable time on repetitive tasks such as manually drafting and formatting documents, saving time, and reducing the potential for errors. Automation streamlines repetitive tasks, freeing up time for higher-value work, which improves overall firm efficiency and reduces human error. It enables faster turnaround for business clients and removes bottlenecks to progress deals faster by improving accessibility to services through self-service while shortening the queue for high importance legal requests.

• *Scalability:* Automation allows law firms to handle growth efficiently, scaling operations without the need for proportional increases in staffing. If your business is growing rapidly or expanding into new markets, legal automation can support with scaling by handling increased legal work without a proportional increase in resources.

• *Competitive Advantage:* Adopting automation positions your firm as innovative, attracting clients looking for efficient and modern legal services. Implementing legal automation can give your business a competitive edge by helping you to deliver faster response times, quicker contract negotiations, and improved client satisfaction.

• *Client Satisfaction:* Saving time and money can also help law offices improve services and increase client satisfaction. Using AI to lower the cost of document processing also means firms have the option of passing on the savings and lowering fees in certain cases, which makes legal services accessible to a wider range of people.

Some of these benefits are shown in Figure 3.9 [9].

Improved consistency & standardisation

Reduced risk

Saved time and faster turnaround times

Reduced costs

Allows lawyers to focus on higher value work

Improved client relationships

Figure 3.9 Some of the benefits of legal automation [9].

3.6 CHALLENGES

There are complex workflows, legal logic, and calculations in legal documents that AI alone cannot solve, just as there are things that automation alone cannot solve. As reliance on technology grows, so does the importance of data privacy and security in legal tech. Ethical concerns about bias in AI models, data privacy, and regulatory compliance must be continuously addressed. It is important to remain vigilant about potential bias in AI-generated documents. In the fierce market competition, law firms today must deal with double-sided demands to become more accessible by cost reduction, but also to provide more effective services to clients. Other challenges of legal automation include the following [6]:

- *Security:* Legal automation platforms must use robust encryption methods to protect sensitive client and case data from unauthorized access. End-to-end encryption ensures that confidential information remains secure both in transit and at rest. With increasing cyber threats looming like dark clouds on the horizon, law firms must prioritize robust security measures. AI plays a pivotal role in enhancing data security protocols within law firms.

- *Regulations:* Automation tools should comply with key data protection regulations such as GDPR, CCPA, and industry-specific legal standards. Firms should ensure that their chosen solutions provide built-in compliance features that align with legal and ethical obligations. With rising regulations around data governance, complete automation software also should include advanced security tools and ensure nothing leaves the company and software/cloud ecosystem.

- *Access Control:* Law firms must implement strict access control measures, ensuring that only authorized personnel can view, edit, or approve automated legal documents. Role-based access and audit trails help maintain accountability and prevent unauthorized changes. The shift to remote work highlighted the value of online practice management systems like Clio. Remote access enables lawyers to view client and matter information, generate documents, and work effectively from anywhere—making it invaluable for solicitors on the go.

- *Transparency:* If AI is used in automation, firms must ensure transparency in how algorithms make decisions. Legal professionals should be able to review and verify AI-generated content to prevent potential errors or biases in automated workflows.

3.7 CONCLUSION

Legal automation keeps evolving and expanding into more areas of legal practice. It has become an essential tool that modern law firms must embrace to stay competitive. Embracing legal automation today can transform your firm's operations, creating a smoother, faster, and more client-focused workflow. The firms that proactively integrate legal automation into their processes will gain a strategic edge in an industry that is increasingly digital. There is now an abundance of secure and reliable AI tools for automating document generation, redaction, analysis, and more.

With advances in artificial intelligence (AI), robotic process automation (RPA), and no-code platforms, legal automation is not just an emerging trend; it is a must-have tool for law firms that want to stay competitive. Automation is not here to replace lawyers; it is here to make them more effective. More information on legal automation is available from the books in [12,13].

REFERENCE

[1] J. Jacinto, "Legal document automation: A complete guide," July 2024,

https://flowtrics.com/legal-document-automation-guide/

[2] S. Lim, "A beginner's guide to legal automation," May 2021.

https://lawgazette.com.sg/practice/tech-talk/a-beginners-guide-to-legal-automation/

[3] G. Garman, "Building a profitable law firm using automation,"

https://www.lawclerk.legal/blog/building-a-profitable-law-firm-using-automation/

[4] M. N. O. Sadiku, P. A. Adekunte, and J. O. Sadiku, "Legal automation," *International Journal of Trend in Scientific Research and Development, vol. 9, no. 2*, March-April 2025, pp. 1335-1343.

[5] "How legal workflow automation turns thousands of tasks into one," May 2023.

https://legal.thomsonreuters.com/blog/how-automation-turns-thousands-of-tasks-into-one/

[6] J. Seduski, "How legal automation is changing everyday work for law firms,"

February 2025,

https://www.templafy.com/legal-document-automation/

[7] T. Litify, "Automation: How law firms get more done with less,"

https://www.litify.com/blog/how-your-law-firm-can-get-more-done-in-less-time-with-process-automation

[8] "Legal document automation: The complete guide for 2025,"

https://erbis.com/blog/legal-document-automation/

[9] "Definitive guide to legal document automation for in-house,"

https://legalsolutions.thomsonreuters.co.uk/en/explore/definitive-guides/document-automation-in-house.html

[10] "What is legal automation?" May 2023,

https://www.checkbox.ai/blog/what-is-legal-automation

[11] E. Bogin, "What is legal document automation, and why is it the new business standard?" August 2024,

https://mitratech.com/resource-hub/blog/what-is-legal-document-automation-and-why-is-it-the-new-business-standard/

[12] P. Wahlgren, *Automation of Legal Reasoning (Computer/Law Series)*. Springer, 1992.

[13] A. Bailey, *AI and the Legal Field: Automation, Ethics, and Intellectual Property*. Independently Published, 2023.

CHAPTER 4
VIRTUAL LEGAL ASSISTANT

"Man is still the most extraordinary computer of all."

—John F. Kennedy

4.1 INTRODUCTION

It takes hard work to run a law firm. It is not possible for the company to handle all the legal affairs by itself. Lawyers often experience workplace stress, which leads to a lack of work-life balance and poor management. They are been overwhelmed with the sheer amount of work involved with running a legal practice. They spend an average of 2.3 hours of their billable day on actual legal work. The rest is consumed by admin tasks that drain productivity and limit revenue potential. Having administrative support can make the difference between being ready for your next case and becoming overburdened. More and more law firms are choosing virtual legal assistants to handle these routine but essential tasks. Virtual legal assistants (VLAs) are responsible for handling repetitive but essential tasks, such as transcription, file management, legal research, email and call handling, and client scheduling. With a legal virtual assistant handling these tasks, your team can focus on what matters most. These knowledgeable individuals offer remote support, handling administrative duties, and offering invaluable assistance to legal practitioners as the world becomes more interconnected.

The digital age has revolutionized the workspace, and virtual legal assistants are becoming a crucial part of this change in the legal field. The emergence of legal virtual assistants in the legal industry represents a transformative shift in how legal practices operate. These experts provide specialized remote services and support, allowing lawyers to focus on core legal tasks and client needs. The responsibilities of a virtual assistant for attorneys extend to managing client calls, coordinating meetings, and overseeing contract management. Figure 4.1 shows a team of attorneys [1].

Figure 4.1 A team of attorneys [1].

A virtual legal assistant (VLA) is a skilled professional who provides remote assistance to legal practitioners and law firms. They provide remote administrative, technical, and legal support to lawyers or law firms, handling tasks like document management, scheduling, client communication, and legal research, freeing up attorneys for core legal work. VLAs are transforming the legal industry by bringing a new level of efficiency and expertise. With a rapid development of law firms, legal virtual assistants have been in much demand because they play a major role in analyzing significant legal documents, drafting various contracts and agreements for the company, handling different case laws, managing the paperwork of the firm, etc. [2].

This chapter examines how virtual legal assistants improve productivity and free up legal professionals to concentrate on what they do best. The chapter begins with explaining what virtual legal assistant is. It discusses various uses of virtual legal assistant. It highlights the benefits and challenges of virtual legal assistant. The last section concludes with comments.

4.2 WHAT IS A VIRTUAL LEGAL ASSISTANT?

The landscape of the legal industry is changing rapidly. The legal profession seeks new and innovative ways to streamline operations and provide the best possible client services. One increasingly popular option is hiring virtual assistants. A virtual legal assistant is a remote professional who provides legal and administrative support to law firms, handling tasks such as scheduling, correspondence, document preparation, and client management, without being physically present in the office. In addition to basic administrative duties, virtual assistants for lawyers often take on roles that require legal research, document drafting, and case management.

Virtual legal assistants, also known as virtual paralegals, support lawyers by organizing legal documents, conducting research, and assisting during trials and hearings. The major difference between a virtual and in-house paralegal is that virtual paralegals work remotely. In-house paralegals could be full-time, part-time, or contract staff, while virtual paralegals mostly work on a freelance or contract basis [3]. They work from their own offices or homes, while in-house paralegals work within a law firm or legal department's physical office. VLAs work closely with attorneys to take care of some of the time-consuming administrative work that reduces lawyer efficiency and productivity. Figure 4.2 shows a typical virtual legal assistant [1].

Figure 4.2 A typical virtual legal assistant [1].

Think of a virtual legal assistant as an extension of yourself for administrative tasks, allowing you to focus on lawyering and billable work. The primary responsibility of a legal assistant is to provide law and legal assistance to the team and support with administrative tasks like organizing documents and files, managing schedules, handling correspondence, conducting research, and drafting and proofreading legal documents. Virtual legal assistants typically have legal experience and are familiar with legal terminology, procedures, and documentation. Figure 4.3 presents must-have skills for a virtual legal assistant [4]. The minimum educational requirement for virtual legal assistants is a high school diploma or GED, though many hold bachelor's or master's degrees.

MUST-HAVE SKILLS FOR A VIRTUAL LEGAL ASSISTANT

- ✓ Organization
- ✓ Legal terminology
- ✓ Time management skills
- ✓ Time management skills
- ✓ Managing emails
- ✓ IT Skills
- ✓ Confidentiality
- ✓ Confidentiality
- ✓ Written Skills

Figure 4.3 Must-have skills for a virtual legal assistant [4].

VLAs handle various administrative tasks such as calendar management, appointment scheduling, document organization, and correspondence drafting. They conduct in-depth legal research, compiling pertinent statutes, rules, and other legal resources. They can represent attorneys in client communications and act as a point of contact for clients [4]. A VLA can act as a communicator between the client and the law firm. It will provide the lawyer assistance in preparing for trials.

Here are some key ways a virtual legal assistant can support your practice [5].

- Assisting with legal research
- Calendar management and schedulin.
- Compiling reports and summaries
- Confirming meetings and setting appointment.
- Email handling and outreach
- Handling client intake
- Keeping up with client communicatio.
- Managing online files
- Updating documents and presentation.
- Inbox management
- Onboarding new clients
- Liaison with intake specialists
- Systems creation
- Data analysis
- Naming electronic files and organizing them
- Sending out retainer agreements and retainer invoice
- Accounts receivable and payable
- Setting up new matters in case management software
- Uploading expenses into bookkeeping software
- Adding people to mailing lists

Figure 4.4 shows those who need legal virtual assistant [4] , while Figure 4.5 shows a snapshot of the legal specialties VLAs can work with [6].

Figure 4.4 Those who need legal virtual assistant [4].

- Corporate Law
- Criminal Law
- Family Law
- Personal Injury Law
- Estate Planning & Probate Law
- Intellectual Property Law
- Real Estate Law

- Employment and Labor Law
- Immigration Law
- Bankruptcy Law
- Tax Law
- Environmental Law
- Healthcare Law

Figure 4.5 A snapshot of the legal specialties VLAs can work with [6].

4.3 USES OF VIRTUAL LEGAL ASSISTANT

A legal assistant completes necessary routine tasks on behalf of a lawyer. The job often includes elements of administration, customer service, and coordination. Lawyers or law firms hire virtual legal assistants to handle the repetitive but essential tasks of a law office, including transcription, file management, legal research, email and call handling, and the like. Tasks to outsource to legal virtual assistants include the following [7]:

• *Administrative Tasks:* Virtual legal assistants are remote professionals who provide essential administrative support to law firms without being physically present in the office. Virtual legal assistants support attorneys with various administrative tasks such as scheduling, correspondence, document preparation, making travel arrangements, coordinating meetings, and providing general administrative support. Virtual legal assistant services are used by law firms, whether that be for legal research, drafting documents, managing cases, or communicating with clients. A virtual legal assistant is not just an administrative helper. They play a crucial role in ensuring that legal operations run efficiently.

• *Sort Through Emails:* Chances are there are lots of unread emails. A VLA will go through your work emails and notify you of important correspondence. The virtual legal assistant will respond to client inquiries as they sort through the emails. Your virtual legal assistant crafts newsletters and emails to keep your clients informed and engaged, ensuring your messages stand out in crowded inboxes.

• *Respond to Inquiries:* First impressions count, especially when potential clients contact your firm. Your virtual assistant is your frontliner, handling initial client inquiries professionally and efficiently. As a lawyer, you have clients to meet, witnesses to interview, and proceedings to attend. The virtual legal assistant will make sure you are aware of all the inquiries and how they were handled just so they will not be left in the dark.

• *Manage Your Calendar:* Calendar management typically means booking, rescheduling, and reminding clients of appointments. Calendaring requires precise attention to detail, keen listening skills, articulate communication about availability, expectations, and associated costs. It may also include light outreach to clients who are due in court to ensure they appear on time and are presentable. It will be your remote legal assistant's duty to manage your calendar and keep you on track. VLAs can handle all aspects of calendar management, including court dates, deadlines, and appointments, ensuring you never miss an important event. They will make sure you do not miss meetings, appointments, and important deadlines by reminding you of your schedule. Having an organized calendar will also help the VLA keep track of your activities so they can make changes if necessary.

• *Organize Files:* The virtual legal assistant is tasked with keeping all the files organized. Lawyers cannot afford to lose or misplace even one document. The files should be accessible from any device so you can take a look whenever and wherever you are.

• *Draft Contracts:* A contract is a set of promises that is legally binding. It ensures that the parties involved will stay true to what has been agreed upon. A contract can be a verbal agreement but this can easily be disputed. The virtual legal assistant will help draft contracts using the details you will provide.

• *Create Presentations:* Lawyers often rely on presentations to communicate their capability to prospective clients. Your chances of you representing them may depend on how clear and impressive your presentation is. The virtual legal assistant may assist you by creating PowerPoint presentations that convey your message with less text and more graphs, figures, and other visuals.

• *Assist in Pre-trial Preparations:* The virtual legal assistant will provide the lawyer assistance in preparing for trials. They will be tasked with writing reports, drafting contracts, and other legal documents necessary in a case. The VLA may also be asked to procure documents that will be used as evidence such as affidavits and formal statements. A bilingual virtual assistant can streamline your law firm's operations, improve client communication, and help you reach new markets.

• *Conduct Research:* There is a bit of investigation involved in law practice. Much of the investigation will be done through thorough legal research. Proper research is vital to a case and while lawyers gain that skill from law school and during practice, they cannot find everything they need all at once. The virtual legal assistant can aid the lawyer by doing some of the necessary research. They conduct thorough legal research, summarizing findings to support your cases effectively, and give you clear summaries, so you can focus on analysis and strategy.

• *Legal Education:* In the field of legal education, a VLA can assist with curriculum management, student communication, and administrative tasks, ensuring smooth operations. Virtual assistants support online schooling systems and assist in research and recruitment, benefiting educational institutions.

• *Invoicing and Billing:* The virtual legal assistant may count billing and invoicing as one of their duties. The VLA can prepare the attorney invoice and send the billing documents to the clients after you have reviewed them.

• *Website Management:* Lawyers need to market themselves and their firms so people are aware of the services they are offering. A website is one tool that can help lawyers and small firms get noticed. The remote assistant will be responsible for maintaining the website. The virtual legal assistant needs to update the website regularly.

• *Customer Support:* Customer support for attorneys often takes the shape of providing case updates, answering and returning calls, replying to emails, monitoring social media, monitoring reviews and requesting them from clients, and triaging communications in general. Monitoring is an essential responsibility of firm owners placing legal virtual assistants in frontline service roles.

4.4 BENEFITS

One of the main benefits of hiring legal virtual assistants is their ability to integrate smoothly into your team. Unlike traditional assistants tied to a specific location, legal virtual assistants can operate from anywhere. Virtual legal assistants remotely provide legal support and assistance to their clients. A virtual legal assistant can be an asset to a legal practice by offering flexible assistance, increased productivity, and other valuable support, enabling attorneys to focus on core work. Other benefits of bringing a legal virtual assistant into your practice include the following [5,8]:

• *Working From Home:* This is typically one of the most commonly named advantages of being a virtual paralegal. When you work from home, you can spend more with your family and avoid the daily commute, dress code, and work schedules associated with working in an office.

• *Increased Productivity:* Virtual legal assistants can help your firm run smoother by handling administrative tasks. This frees up your in-house team to concentrate on the work that really matters. VLAs manage your calendar, emails, and documents, letting lawyers focus on legal matters.

• *Cost Savings:* One of the biggest advantages is cost savings. Hiring a virtual assistant can be significantly cheaper than employing full-time, in-house staff. You can save on expenses typically associated with full-time staff, which means more budget for client services. No need to pay for office space or supplies. Research shows that it can cost as low as $17 per hour for a virtual assistant, while in-house alternatives may cost around $25 per hour. VLAs typically work on a contract basis, which means law firms can save on overhead costs such as office space, equipment, and benefits.

• *Better Client Satisfaction:* Hiring a legal virtual assistant can lead to happier clients through improved communication and responsiveness. LVAs ensure clients receive timely updates on their cases.

• *Remote Efficiency:* The remote nature of their work offers flexibility and adaptability, aligning with various legal practice models and needs. This adaptability is particularly beneficial for legal practices looking to scale or adjust their operations quickly.

• *Flexibility:* Another great advantage of hiring legal virtual assistants is their flexibility. VLAs are trained to be flexible and adaptable to varying workloads, which can be particularly beneficial for smaller firms that lack the resources to hire full-time staff to manage fluctuating workloads. Their flexibility lets you quickly adapt to changes in the market. As your practice evolves, the flexibility of legal virtual assistants ensures you have the support you need when it matters most. Flexibility and adaptability allow virtual legal assistants to remain effective and productive, even in fast-paced and unpredictable environments.

• *Scalability:* Virtual assistants can scale services easily with business requirements. They can grow or shrink with business needs. They are ideal for startups and small businesses aiming to expand efficiently. As your practice grows or fluctuates, virtual assistants can easily be scaled up or down to fit your needs. You can adjust the number of assistants based on the current workload.

• *Embracing Technology:* Stay ahead with tech-savvy virtual legal assistants ready to implement innovative tools to streamline your operations. They can automate routine tasks, boosting efficiency, and reducing errors.

• *Gaining a Competitive Edge:* In a crowded legal market, leveraging virtual legal assistants can give your firm a leg up. Enhanced efficiency and top-notch service can help you stand out. With help of LVAs, your firm operates more efficiently, strengthens client relationships, and excels in a competitive landscape.

• *Collaboration:* Technological advancements can allow a virtual legal assistant to collaborate seamlessly with attorneys or other legal team members regardless of location, communicating and managing workflows through video conferencing tools, project management solutions, and document-sharing platforms. Collaborating effectively with VLAs requires clear communication and proper management.

• *Effective Communication:* Effective communication is essential to a successful collaboration with a formal legal assistant. Establish clear guidelines on preferred communication channels, response times, and project updates. Use email, instant messaging, and project management systems to communicate consistently and transparently. VLAs can handle client communications, ensuring that inquiries and concerns are addressed promptly. This leads to higher client satisfaction and loyalty. VLA provides effective communication as shown in Figure 4.6 [9].

Figure 4.6 VLA provides effective communication [9].

• *Time Management:* Effective time management is a vital quality for the best virtual legal assistant, as illustrated in Figure 4.7 [9]. In a profession where deadlines are critical, being able to prioritize and manage time efficiently ensures that tasks are completed on schedule and to a high standard. With excellent time management skills, a virtual legal assistant can help law firms meet deadlines, avoid delays, and maintain smooth operations.

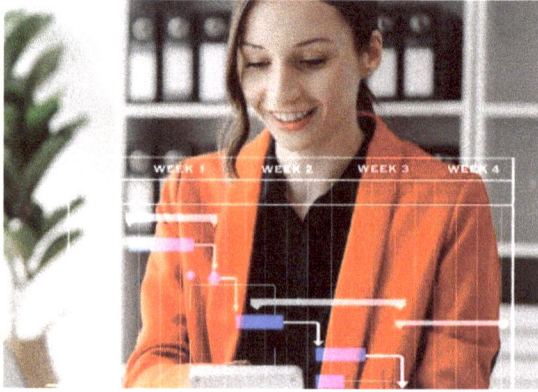

Figure 4.7 Effective time management is a vital quality for the best VLA [9].

Some of these benefits are shown in Figure 4.8 [4].

BENEFITS OF HIRING A VIRTUAL LEGAL ASSISTANT

Efficiency and Cost-effectiveness

Flexibility and Scalability

Improved Work-life Balance

Enhanced Client Service

Confidentiality and Data Security

Increased Competitive Advantage

Figure 4.8 Some benefits of a virtual legal assistant [4].

4.5 CHALLENGES

Disadvantages of VLA include potential communication challenges, data security concerns, and the need for clear communication and expectations to ensure effective collaboration. Though legal assistants can take on many support and administrative tasks on behalf of a lawyer, legal assistants are limited in what they can do. Non-lawyer legal staff like legal assistants cannot under any circumstances practice law, give clients legal advice, or present themselves as lawyers. Supervising lawyers must make reasonable efforts to ensure non-lawyers that they employ conduct themselves in ways that align with the lawyer's professional obligations. Other challenges or disadvantages of VLA include the following [3,8,10]:

• *No Benefits:* As an independent virtual paralegal, you do not have health insurance, retirement, paid vacation, paid sick leave or other benefits that you may have if you work for an attorney. If you are a virtual paralegal employed by a law firm, you may have these benefits.

• *Increasing Competition:* Virtual paralegals are growing in numbers as individuals look to own their own business, spend more time with their family and be in more control of their career. While the opportunities for virtual paralegals arc growing as attorneys seek to reduce overhead costs, the competition for those jobs are increasing as more paralegals choose to go "virtual" with their career.

• *Data Security:* The legal profession deals with highly sensitive and confidential information, and virtual assistants must be entrusted with this information. Remote work introduces potential security risks, including data breaches or unauthorized access, requiring robust security protocols and careful selection of virtual assistants. Sharing of sensitive legal information and documents gives rise to security concerns. Protect sensitive customer information and legal documents by implementing strong security measures. Your legal virtual assistant must sign a confidentiality agreement outlining their responsibility to protect client privacy and data. Regularly review and update your security measures to meet regulatory standards and protect sensitive information within your legal operations.

• *Regulations:* Specific codes, rules, and regulations for working with legal assistants may vary depending on your jurisdiction. It is important to check and abide by your state's rules and regulations for how lawyers may work with and what duties they can assign to legal assistants.

• *Communication Challenges:* Virtual assistants are not physically present in the office, which can lead to communication and coordination difficulties, impacting real-time problem-solving and collaboration. If the virtual assistant is in a different time zone, this can further complicate communication and lead to delays and disruptions.

• *Technical Challenges:* Virtual assistants rely heavily on technology, and technical issues like Internet outages or software problems can disrupt work and communication, affecting productivity. Ensuring that the virtual assistant's software and hardware are compatible with the law firm's systems can be a challenge.

• *Building Relationships:* Building a strong working relationship with a virtual assistant can be more challenging than with in-house staff, as personal connections and rapport may take longer to establish. Clear and effective communication and expectations are key to overcoming this challenge and ensuring a smooth workflow.

4.6 CONCLUSION

The legal industry today is concerned about being efficient and accurate. Virtual assistants have become a game changer in the legal industry, helping lawyers improve their efficiency and accuracy. The role of a legal virtual assistant is dynamic and indispensable. Virtual legal assistants are leading the charge in the digital transformation of the legal industry, revolutionizing traditional business models through the implementation of artificial intelligence. They are reshaping the legal landscape by helping firms gain a competitive edge, streamline workflows, and offer more personalized services to their clients. They have been positively transforming the legal industry over the past few years, providing cost-effective, flexible, and efficient support to law firms of all sizes [11]. More information about virtual legal assistants can be found in the books in [12-15].

REFERENCE

[1] "How virtual legal assistants are transforming the legal industry,.

https://www.virtuallatinos.com/blog/virtual-legal-assistants-industry/

[2] M. N. O. Sadiku, P. A. Adekunte, and J. O. Sadiku, "Virtual legal assistant," *International Journal of Trend in Scientific Research and Development*, vol. 9, no. 2, March-April 2025, pp. 565-573.

[3] R. Kaushal, "Hiring a virtual paralegal: Weighing the pros and cons," February 2025,

https://www.legalsupportworld.com/blog/virtual-paralegal-services-pros-and-cons/

[4] "Guide to virtual legal assistant for attorneys and law firms,"

https://www.wishup.co/blog/virtual-legal-assistant/

[5] "The advantages of hiring a virtual legal assistants," November 2024,

https://attorneyassistant.com/the-advantages-of-hiring-a-virtual-legal-assistant/

[6] "US-based virtual legal assistants,"

https://virtualgalfriday.com/virtual_assistant_services/virtual-legal-assistant.html

[7] D. J. Tality, "Virtual legal assistant services in Mexico: An affordable solution," March 2025,

https://20four7va.com/client-tips/virtual-legal-assistant/

[8] T. Pierce, "The pros and cons of being a virtual paralegal," https://www.agilelaw.com/blog/pros-cons-virtual-paralegal/

[9] 'Virtual legal assistant (VLA),"

https://www.apcallcenters.com/services/virtual-solutions/virtual-legal-assistant-vla/

[10] S. Miki, "What is a legal assistant? Their role and how it helps lawyers,"

https://www.clio.com/blog/what-is-a-legal-assistant/

[11] "How virtual legal assistants are transforming the legal industry,"

https://www.virtuallatinos.com/blog/virtual-legal-assistants-industry/

[12] D. E. Larbalestrier and L. Spagnola, *Paralegal Practice & Procedure Fourth Edition: A Practical Guide for the Legal Assistant*. Penguin Publishing Group, 2009.

[13] H. Jo, *Hiring the Right VA and Becoming a Virtual Assistant: A guide for the Entrepreneur and the Virtual Assistant Who Are Looking For One Another But Have No Idea Where To Start!* Independently Published, 2024.

[14] C. Charvis, *Virtual Paralegal Entrepreneurs: The Blueprint for Using Your Paralegal Skills to Launch a Business*. VPE Publishing, 2023.

[15] J. Holders, *Virtual Assistant: Jobs, Companies, Services, Training, and Salary*. Self Publisher, 2024.

CHAPTER 5
CLOUD COMPUTING IN LAW PRACTICE

"Morality cannot be legislated, but behavior can be regulated. Judicial decrees may not change the heart, but they can restrain the heartless."

—Martin Luther King, Jr.

5.1 INTRODUCTION

The recent emergence of cloud computing is one of the major advances in the history of computing. Cloud computing is a computing paradigm for delivering computing services (such as servers, storage, databases, networking, software, analytics, and more) over the "the cloud" with pay-as-you-go pricing. The term "cloud" denotes "the Internet," so that "cloud computing" is also called "Internet computing." Cloud computing is a means of pooling and sharing hardware and software resources on a massive scale. Users and businesses can access applications from anywhere in the world at any time. Companies offering these computing services are called cloud providers and typically charge for cloud computing services based on usage [1]. In a rapidly evolving digital world, the legal profession is not immune to the transformative power of the cloud computing technology. Figure 5.1 show a picture relating to the word cloud for cloud computing [2]. Some features of cloud computing are displayed in Figure 5.2 [3].

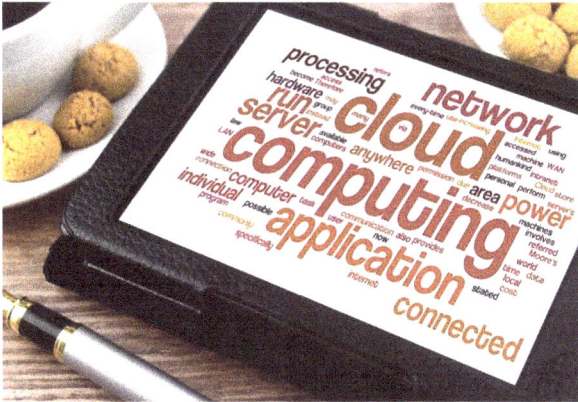

Figure 5.1 The word cloud for cloud computing [2].

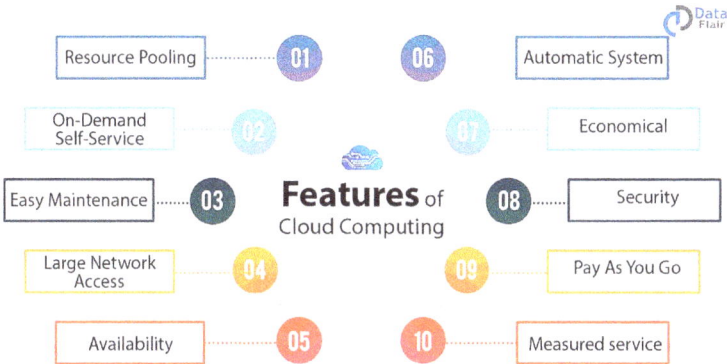

Figure 5.2 Some features of cloud computing [3].

Cloud computing has long since ceased to be the future and has become the reality of the legal sector. Rather than building, owning, and maintaining their own IT infrastructure, legal businesses can use cloud to access technology resources such as computing capacity, storage, and databases on a pay-as-you-go basis. An industry needs the cloud for the following reasons: (1) Mobile workforce: empowering employees to sift real time data and make decisions on the fly, (2) Minimize disruptions: with the right sort of cloud setup problems can be anticipated and solved quickly, (3) Collaboration: with the right technology, collaboration – as well as transparency and accountability – are easily managed, (4) Innovation: product innovation and process innovation are powerful weapons to survive or thrive in such an environment, (5) Lower cost: No hardware procurement, maintenance, or staff is needed to operate the systems.

Cloud computing is the future of the next generation computing systems in the world. Organizations with not enough resources to build their own infrastructure can now take advantage of the cloud services to suit their specific needs. Cloud computing is transforming industries, and the legal sector is no exception. Cloud computing in law refers to the legal framework and regulations governing the use of cloud services, encompassing data privacy, security, intellectual property, and jurisdictional issues. The era of cloud computing has just begun, and the time is soon approaching when the use of physical memory devices will become obsolete [4,5].

This chapter considers how cloud computing is revolutionizing legal practice. The chapter begins with explaining the basics of cloud computing. It discusses cloud computing in law and its applications. It highlights the benefits and challenges of cloud computing in law. The last section concludes with comments.

5.2 CLOUD COMPUTING BASICS

Cloud computing represents a newly emerging service-oriented computing technology. It is the provision of scalable computing resources as a service over the Internet. It allows manufacturers to use many forms of new production systems such as 3D printing, high-performance computing (HPC), industrial Internet of things (IIoT), and industrial robots. It is transforming virtually every facet of modern manufacturing. It is innovating, reducing cost, and bolstering the competitiveness of American manufacturing [6]. Figure 5.3 shows the symbol for cloud computing [7].

Figure 5.3 The symbol for cloud computing [7].

The key characteristic of cloud computing is the virtualization of computing resources and services. Cloud computing is implemented in one of three major formats: software as a service (SAAS), platform as a service (PAAS), or infrastructure as a service (IAAS). These services are illustrated in Figure 5.4 [8] and explained as follows:

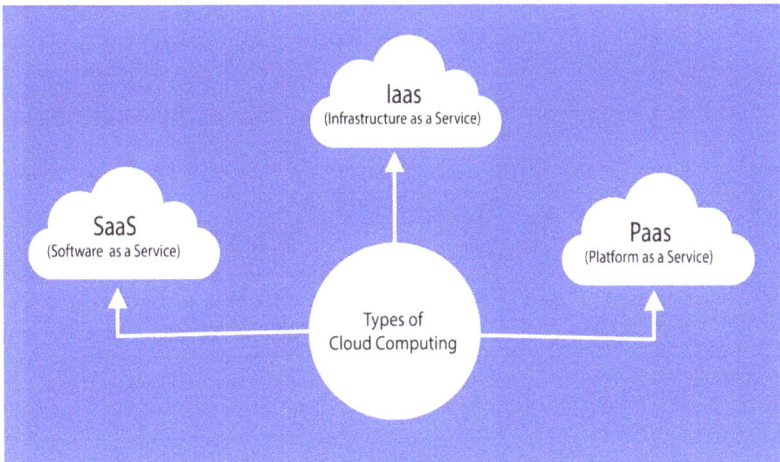

Figure 5.4 Three types of cloud computing [8].

SaaS: This is a software delivery model in which software and associated data are hosted on the cloud. In this model, cloud service providers offer on-demand access to computing resources such as virtual machines and cloud storage.

PaaS allows the end-user to create a software solution using tools or libraries from the platform service provider. In this model, cloud service providers deliver computing platforms such as programming and execution.

In the IaaS model, cloud service providers can rent manufacturing equipment such as 3D printers.

Just like cloud computing, CM services can be categorized into three major deployment models (public, private, and hybrid clouds) [9]:

- Private cloud refers to a centralized management effort in which manufacturing services are shared within one company or its subsidiaries. A private cloud is often used exclusively by one organization, possibly with multiple business units.

- Public cloud realizes the key concept of sharing services with the general public. Public clouds are commonly implemented through data centers operated by providers such as Amazon, Google, IBM, and Microsoft.

- Hybrid cloud that spans multiple configurations and is a composed of two or more clouds (private, community or public), offering the benefits of multiple deployment modes.

These models are shown in Figure 5.5 [10]. Cloud computing finds application in almost every field.

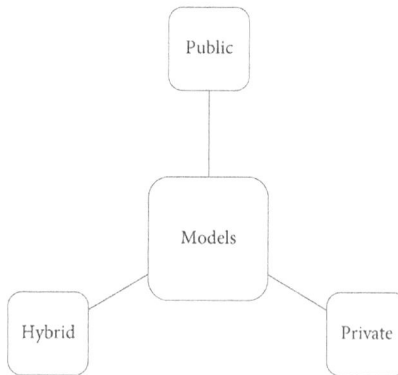

Figure 5.5 Cloud computing models [10].

5.3 CLOUD COMPUTING IN LAW

Technology is changing much faster than law. Professionals and law firms must transform themselves in order to offer better and more efficient services in an eminently technological society. The cloud enables users to set up a hard drive and securely run software on the Internet, giving them access to essential data, applications, and tools anytime from anywhere – a law office, coffee shop, home office, or even the kitchen table. The use of cloud computing systems and services is becoming more and more widespread as law firms discover how efficient and streamlined they can make their practice. Cloud computing is yet another example of how technology, far from replacing lawyers with robots or machines, helps to improve efficiency. Some benefits of moving to the cloud include stronger security, increased flexibility for remote work, and more scalability.

There are generally no laws directly applicable to cloud computing. However, there are numerous federal and state laws and regulations that may indirectly impact the use of cloud computing applications and use cases. With regard to those laws that may indirectly impact the use of cloud computing, a breach of such laws can result in a variety of consequences such as fines and penalties. For example, there is a patchwork of federal and state privacy laws that may impact the application of cloud computing. Data privacy and security requirements at the state level vary significantly, with breach notification laws in all 50 states. US customers with international operations remain subject to international privacy laws. The procurement of goods and services by state and local governmental bodies is governed by the procurement laws of the state in question. One would wish that there were a set of laws for all nations across the globe. Unfortunately, there generally are not any consumer laws that are directly applicable to cloud computing [11].

5.4 APPLICATIONS OF CLOUD COMPUTING IN LAW

Cloud computing is a new computing paradigm and is often synonymous with Internet computing, cluster computing, grid computing, utility computing, P2P computing, service computing, market-oriented computing, and Web 2.0. It is now a concept that is familiar to most lawyers. Examples of successful implementations of cloud computing in law firms can be seen across a variety of legal organizations. Popular cloud applications support streamlined case management, time tracking, billing, client intake, and collaboration. Some applications of cloud computing in the legal sector are presented as follows:

• *Cloud Computing Law:* Cloud computing law refers to the legal framework and regulations that govern the use of cloud computing services. It deals with the legal issues that arise when business and personal assets are stored and processed in the cloud. The law encompasses various aspects such as data privacy, security, intellectual property rights, jurisdictional issues, and contractual agreements between cloud service providers and their clients. The US does not have one all-encompassing law for data regulation across the country. However, US government makes efforts to protect public safety and combat serious crime, including terrorism. Figure 5.6 represents cloud computing in law [12].

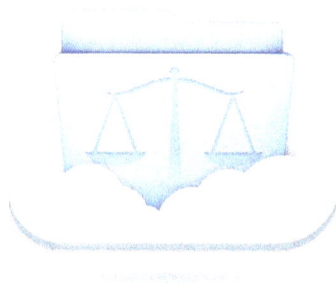

Figure 5.6 Representation of cloud computing in law [12]..

• *Managed Cloud Services:* As the legal industry continues to embrace digital transformation, the demand for managed cloud services for law firms is poised to grow exponentially. Managed cloud services offer law firms a strategic approach to leveraging cloud technology, providing comprehensive support for infrastructure management, security, compliance, and optimization. With managed cloud services for law firms, you can offload the burden of managing and maintaining your cloud infrastructure to experienced professionals, allowing you to focus on your core business objectives.

• *Law Enforcement:* Law enforcement officials have many responsibilities, such as deterring crime, patrolling assigned areas, monitoring activities to protect people and property, responding to emergencies, etc. Across the nation, they are using the cloud for a variety of functions, such as data backup and disaster recovery. This technology can also be useful in other ways, such as by organizing and storing large amounts of digital media files and evidence. In the law enforcement industry, the challenge of securely managing an ever-growing accumulation of data while keeping it accessible in a mobile environment is accelerating at a rapid speed. Law enforcement officials manage a large volume of personally identifiable information, arrest records, background reports, and other private data considered to be sensitive and confidential information. To protect the privacy of certain individuals, law enforcement is responsible for handling this information in a manner that is secure, ethical, and sensitive. Failure to comply with certain federal policies can result in hefty fines or other legal implications for agencies found at fault. Switching to cloud-based computing can save law enforcement departments a large amount of money over time [13].

• *Documentation:* Documentation is a significant part of a lawyer's profession. Using cloud storage platforms is a great way for a law firm to safely share documents with clients or associates. Legal professionals often deal with voluminous data. Cloud computing offers a scalable solution, adapting to the size and requirements of any legal firm. Not only does it provide an efficient way to store data, but its accessibility makes data retrieval a seamless process, even from remote locations.

• *Data Ownership:* In today's digital age, data has become a valuable asset for businesses across various industries. The collection, storage, and analysis of vast amounts of data have revolutionized the way organizations operate and make informed decisions. Who owns the data that is generated and collected? What are the rights associated with this data? These questions have sparked debates and discussions among experts and policymakers. Data ownership refers to the legal and ethical concept that determines who has control and authority over data. It involves identifying the individual or entity that possesses the right to determine how data is collected, stored, used, and shared. When it comes to data ownership, different perspectives exist, ranging from individual rights to corporate interests. From an individual's standpoint, there is a growing awareness of personal data ownership and the need for control over its usage. From a business perspective, data ownership is often seen as a valuable asset that can provide a competitive advantage. Individuals are increasingly concerned about the ownership and control of their personal data. To address the complexities surrounding data ownership and data rights, various legal frameworks and regulations have been developed globally. These frameworks generally seek to strike a balance between individual privacy rights and business interests [14].

• *Intellectual Property Protection:* Data privacy is not limited to customer information; it also encompasses protecting a company's intellectual property. Businesses invest substantial resources in research and development, creating proprietary algorithms, formulas, and trade secrets. If these valuable assets are compromised due to weak data privacy practices, it can have detrimental effects on a company's competitive advantage and market position. Legal frameworks address the need for data protection and security measures. In some cases, data ownership intersects with intellectual property rights and trade secrets [14].

5.5 BENEFITS

Cloud computing enables decentralized data processing with the centralized storage of data. Such an approach helps mitigate the need to carry storage devices along with the computer. This further lowers the cost of computing devices and makes digital devices much more affordable. The benefits of using cloud computing for law firms are numerous, ranging from increased accessibility to enhanced data security. The many benefits of cloud computing far outweigh the drawbacks. Cloud services seek to enhance efficiency, collaboration, and security. Other benefits of cloud computing in law include the following [14-16]:

• *Cost-effectiveness:* No discussion of the merits of cloud-based services would be complete without addressing the cost savings these platforms deliver for law firms. For starters, cloud computing is more cost-effective, in part because the initial costs of moving to the cloud are far lower than purchasing a server. Cloud computing can be cost-efficient for small businesses, but it can also lead to increased expenditure due to hidden costs. Cloud computing is characterized by five attractive benefits companies can leverage in delivering cost-effective services in the long run. These include the following [10]: (i) On-demand self-service helps the customers avail services without a third party's interference. (ii) Broad cloud network provides universal access to all users across the globe in real-time. (iii) Resource pooling aids the Cloud Service Provider (CSP) to reap economy of scale benefits and provide budget cloud services. (iv) Rapid elasticity allows the customer to utilize the cloud data on-demand as and when required. (v) Measured service permits CSPs to implement a Pay-as-you-go model for their customers.

• *Accessibility:* One of the primary benefits of cloud computing for law firms is the increased accessibility and mobility of data. With cloud computing, lawyers and staff members can access files and documents from anywhere in the world with an Internet connection. They can access company files from a variety of devices, including laptops, desktops, tablets, and mobile phones.

• *Scalability:* Cloud-based computing is easy to scale. Cloud computing offers scalability and flexibility to accommodate changing business needs. As a law firm grows and expands, it may need to scale up its IT infrastructure to meet new demands. Companies can easily scale their computing resources up or down as needed, without making major investments in hardware or infrastructure.

• *Data Storage:* Cloud-based data storage is easier and, usually, cheaper than keeping law firm files on physical servers or in file cabinets. Cloud computing for law firms is a great way to store data because it allows you to access it anywhere in the world. This makes it easy for the legal industry because it eliminates the need for clients to store documents on their servers. Cloud storage options have become increasingly popular among law firms over the years. Cloud computing offers limitless storage capacity, which can eliminate concerns about storage space. Relative to paper filing systems, it's easier and faster to locate documents stored in the cloud. Cloud computing is the future of data storage and access, and law firms are no exception.

• *Collaboration:* Collaboration is essential in law firms, and cloud computing has revolutionized the way lawyers and staff work together. Cloud-based software allows law firms to access shared documents and information from any device with an internet connection and to collaborate in real time with colleagues, regardless of their physical location. Cloud computing allows multiple users to edit and work on one file simultaneously, and many services provide social features for communication and data sharing. With cloud computing, lawyers and staff members can access files and documents from anywhere with an Internet connection. This means that they can work remotely without being tied to their physical office space.

• *Disaster Recovery:* Cloud computing has dramatically changed how we approach data security as cloud computing provides a solution for disaster backup and recovery. Cloud computing makes disaster recovery easier, as vital data is stored off-site in third-party data centers. Cloud providers often have backup systems in place to ensure that data is not lost in the event of a disaster, such as a fire or flood.

• *Protecting Confidentiality:* Client confidentiality is one of the most important aspects of legal practice. Law firms need to ensure that they protect their clients' sensitive information from unauthorized access or disclosure. Cloud-based practice management systems provide secure solutions for protecting client confidentiality. They offer encryption features that ensure that all data transmitted between users is encrypted, making it difficult for unauthorized parties to intercept or steal sensitive information.

• *Efficiency:* Cloud computing saves both time and money. Law firms can take advantage of cloud computing to reduce the cost of their IT administration. By using cloud computing, IT departments can be outsourced to a company that will provide them with access to everything they need without worrying about managing it themselves.

• *Reliability:* Cloud service providers invest heavily in robust infrastructure and redundancy measures to ensure high availability and reliability with their cloud based services for law firms. With cloud-based law firm software, firms can enjoy 24/7 access to their data and applications, with minimal downtime or disruptions.

• *Flexibility:* The dynamic nature of the legal industry demands solutions that can adapt to law firms' ever-changing needs. Cloud computing provides the perfect answer with its hallmark features of scalability and adaptability. Law firms can say goodbye to costly hardware upgrades with cloud computing and embrace a more flexible and cost-effective approach. Cloud-based legal technology like Clio lets lawyers work securely from anywhere with a strong Internet connection. For many lawyers, the flexibility of remote work is no longer a nice-to-have but rather a necessity. Remote work can also work better for lawyers with families, pets, and other commitments.

• *Transparency:* Transparency plays a crucial role in empowering individuals regarding their data rights. Organizations should clearly communicate their data collection practices, including the types of data collected, the purpose behind it, and the duration for which it will be retained. Moreover, individuals should have the ability to exercise control over their data. By providing transparency and control, individuals can actively participate in the data-sharing process and protect their privacy.

• *Data Portability:* Data portability is another aspect that empowers individuals by giving them the freedom to move their data between different platforms or services. This allows individuals to switch providers without losing their valuable data or being locked into a particular system. By enabling data portability, individuals are not only empowered but also encouraged to make choices based on their preferences, fostering competition and innovation among service providers.

Some of these benefits are depicted in Figure 5.7 [17].

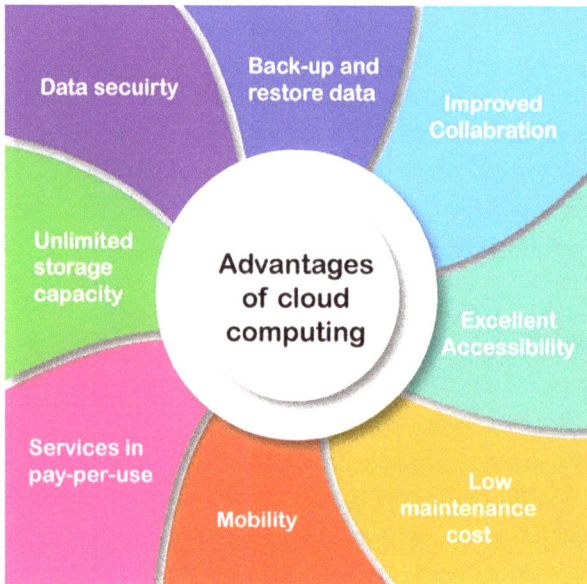

Figure 5.7 Some benefits of cloud computing [17].

5.6 CHALLENGES

Recent years have seen exponential growth in the use of cloud computing to allow greater access to files. While cloud technology offers an impressive range of possibilities, it also creates significant legal challenges for both organizations and individuals. Our laws, largely based on notions of territoriality, struggle to respond to technology in which lines on maps are largely irrelevant. Now more than ever, organizations are migrating workloads to the cloud so they can rapidly scale their business services in order to meet demand. But moving too quickly can cause long-term challenges. It is important to have the right people, processes, and tools in place to maximize success. Internet access is required in order to access your information stored in the cloud. Other challenges of cloud computing in law include the following [14,18].

• *Privacy:* A primary challenge deals with privacy issues associated with the use of data stored in the cloud. Privacy is a big concern when outsourcing your backup, especially with lawyer-client privilege to maintain. Data privacy regulations and vendor agreements are just some of the issues that need to be considered before jumping on the cloud bandwagon. While threats from within and from without do exist, governments create laws that make it possible for malicious individuals or agencies to take advantage of the powers that they grant. It is done in the name of security while taking away your rights to privacy.

• *Security:* The waging cybersecurity challenges have turned cyberspace into cyber warfare in the form of ransomware, distributed denial of services (DDoS), and spyware. Sharing sensitive company data with a third-party cloud service provider can pose a security risk, as hackers may be able to access the information. A reputable cloud solution will be more secure than paper files and files stored on a local server. The cloud application security problems are illustrated in Figure 5.8 [19].

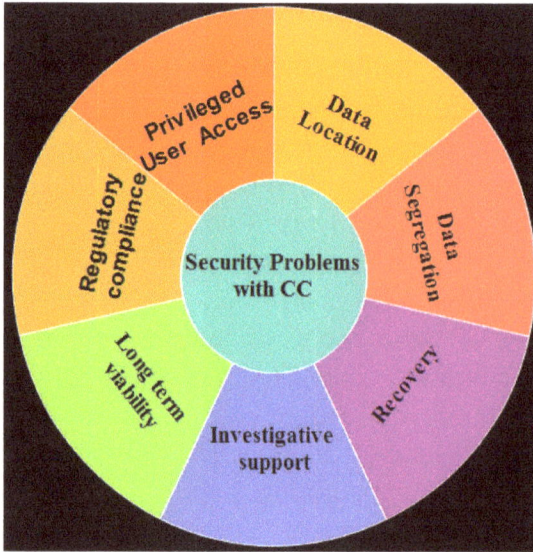

Figure 5.8 Cloud application security problems [19].

• *Ethical Concern:* Ethical concerns may arise when moving client data into the cloud. As the use of cloud computing by lawyers increases, what are the ethical implications for lawyers storing client files remotely? In short, lawyers must observe their long-standing ethical obligation to preserve client confidence and conduct due diligence into any service or vendor used to store client information. The Legal Cloud Computing Association (LCCA) released its security standards providing guidelines for cloud service providers to ensure adequate protection of client data stored in the cloud in a manner consistent with lawyers' ethical obligations. The starting point for legal ethics and cloud computing for lawyers is an attorney's obligation to keep client matters confidential.

• *Regulatory Compliance:* Various jurisdictions have regulations concerning data storage and privacy. Law firms need to ensure their cloud-based operations comply with these regulations. Following good rules and regulations will help create a safe cloud environment. Legal professionals have long been wary about a move to the cloud environment with specific concerns about data privacy regulations at the core of that apprehension. The US does not have one all-encompassing law for data regulation across the country. Instead, it has implemented sector-specific data laws and regulations that work together with state-level legislation in order to keep citizens' data safe, like HIPAA.

• *Resistance to Change:* The legal industry has always been reluctant to move to the cloud. Although resistance to change can be a daunting force in the legal industry, overcoming that resistance is necessary for a successful migration to the cloud. The problem here lies in the fact that companies do not understand the idea of moving to cloud and do not know how to reorganize the existing infrastructure. Legal professionals sometimes believe that migrating to the cloud means giving up control over their data and their critical documents because their servers will not be located nearby.

• *Lack of Clarity:* One of the primary challenges is the lack of clarity surrounding data ownership. With the vast amount of data generated and shared online, it can be difficult to determine who owns the data and what rights they have over it. This ambiguity can lead to disputes and legal complexities.

5.7 CONCLUSION

Cloud computing is a way of delivering computing resources as a utility service via a network, typically the Internet, scalable up and down according to user requirements. It has become one of the most skyrocketing, transformative, and innovative technologies of the 21st century, revolutionizing almost every industry on the planet. The legal industry is rapidly changing, and law firms that want to stay ahead of the curve must embrace cloud computing.

Many businesses have embraced the cloud, especially in recent years, as flexible work arrangements have become the norm. As law firms increasingly use cloud computing for their day-to-day work, managing their infrastructure has become increasingly important. This type of technology has allowed law offices to increase efficiency, streamline workflows, collaborate seamlessly with clients globally, and access resources from anywhere at any time. As technology continues to evolve and the legal industry works hard to stay on top of advancing innovations, cloud computing stands out as a major area of opportunity. More information about cloud computing in law can be found in books in [20-31] and the following related journals.

- *Journal of Cloud Computing*

- *IEEE Cloud Computing*

- *IEEE Transactions on Cloud Computing*

- *International Journal of Cloud Applications and Computing*

- *International Journal of Cloud Computing and Services Science*

- *i-manager's Journal on Cloud Computing*

- *Richmond Journal of Law and Technology*

- *Masaryk University Journal of Law and Technology*

- *Journal of Law and Emerging Technologies*

REFERENCE

[1] M. N. O. Sadiku, S. M. Musa, and O. D. Momoh, "Cloud computing: Opportunities and challenges," IEEE Potentials, January-February 2014, pp. 34-36.

[2] "Creative commons: Tablet word cloud cloud computing image,"

https://www.thebluediamondgallery.com/tablet/c/cloud-computing.html

[3] "Features of cloud computing – 10 major characteristics of cloud computing,"

https://data-flair.training/blogs/features-of-cloud-computing/

[4] M. N. O. Sadiku, C. M. M. Kotteti, and J. O. Sadiku, "Cloud computing law: An introduction," *International Journal of Trend in Research and Development, vol. 11, no. 3*, May-June 2024, pp. 176-179.

[5] M. N. O. Sadiku, P. A. Adekunte, and J. O. Sadiku, "Cloud computing in the legal industry," *International Journal of Trend in Scientific Research and Development, vol. 9, no. 2*, March-April 2025, pp. 574-563.

[6] S. Ezell and B. Swanson, "How cloud computing enables modern manufacturing," June 2017

https://itif.org/publications/2017/06/22/how-cloud-computing-enables-modern-manufacturing

[7] "Stay safe online: Importance of cloud application security," September 2024,

https://litslink.com/blog/cloud-application-security

[8] "Cloud computing applications in agriculture,"

https://www.eescorporation.com/cloud-computing-applications-in-agriculture/

[9] "Cloud manufacturing," Wikipedia, the free encyclopedia

https://en.wikipedia.org/wiki/Cloud_manufacturing

[10] J. S. Saini et al., "[Retracted] cloud computing: Legal issues and provision," *Security and Communication Networks, vol.* 2022,

https://www.hindawi.com/journals/scn/2022/2288961/

[11] "Is cloud computing specifically recognised and provided for in your legal system? If so, how?" September 2023, Unknown Source.

[12] "Cloud benefits attract law firms," February 2016,

https://www.infolaw.co.uk/partners/cloud-benefits-attract-law-firms/

[13] "Top benefits for cloud-based computing in law enforcement," June 2022,

https://www.openfox.com/top-benefits-for-cloud-based-computing-in-law-enforcement/

[14] "Data ownership: Data ownership and data rights for business data privacy," June 2024.

https://fastercapital.com/topics/legal-and-ethical-issues-in-cloud-computing.html

[15] C. Brock, "Why and how are law firms moving to the cloud?" June 2023,

https://www.lawpay.com/about/blog/cloud-computing-for-law-firms/

[16] "5 Reasons your law firm's sensitive data belongs in the cloud," December 2022,

https://natlawreview.com/article/5-reasons-your-law-firm-s-sensitive-data-belongs-cloud

[17] "Advantages and disadvantages of cloud computing,"

https://www.javatpoint.com/advantages-and-disadvantages-of-cloud-computing

[18] "Cloud computing for law firms,"

https://www.binadox.com/blog/cloud-computing-for-law-firms/

[19] https://www.researchgate.net/figure/Security-Issues-in-Cloud-Computing_fig1_326020525

[20] M. N. O. Sadiku, *Cloud Computing and Its Applications.* Moldova, Europe: Lambert Academic Publishing, 2024.

[21] M. N. O. Sadiku, *Law in the Digital Age.* Las Vegas, NV: Book Films Media, 2024.

[22] N. Haughey, *Thinking Out Cloud: Cloud Computing Law.* In Futuro Publishing, 2013.

[23] R. Buyya, J. Broberg, and A. Goscinski (eds.), *Cloud Computing: Principles and Paradigms.* John Wiley & Sons, 2011.

[24] X. Kontargyris, *IT Laws in the Era of Cloud-Computing: A Comparative Analysis Between EU and US Law on the Case Study of Data Protection and Privacy.* Nomos Verlag, 2018.

[25] N. Black, *Cloud Computing for Lawyers. American Bar Association*, 2012.

[26] T. J. Shaw, *Cloud Computing for Lawyers and Executives: A Global Approach.* American Bar Association, 2013.

[27] G. Kaur and R. Malhotra, *Law on Cloud Computing.* Delhi, India: Whitesmann Publishing Co., 2023.

[28] A. S. Y. Cheung and R. H. Weber (eds.), *Privacy and Legal Issues in Cloud Computing.* Edward Elgar Publishing, 2017.

[29] T. Asai, *Artificial Intelligence Self-Driving Cloud Computing and Platforms - Legal Issues of The Fourth Industrial Revolution (Japanese Edition).* Kindle Edition, 2019.

[30] G. Wills, R.J. Walters, and V. Chang, *Delivery and Adoption of Cloud Computing Services in Contemporary Organizations*. IGI Global, 2015.

[31] C. J. Millard (ed.), *Cloud Computing Law*. Oxford, UK: Oxford University Press, 2nd edition, 2021.

CHAPTER 6
IMMERSIVE TECHNOLOGIES IN LAW PRACTICE

"Today's technology makes possible virtual space and virtual operations. A small company does not need expensive offices; some employees can work at home. Key players may live in different cities but be linked electronically. A small company can be a virtual company."

—James Martin

6.1 INTRODUCTION

The legal field is continually evolving, adapting to the changes brought about by technology. As courtroom technology evolves, legal professionals need tools that can keep up. In the ever-evolving landscape of technology, virtual reality (VR) stands as a pinnacle of innovation, propelling users into realms of immersive experiences previously confined to the realms of imagination. This digital marvel is a technology that immerses users in a computer-generated environment, allowing them to interact with it as if it were real. VR is reshaping the landscape of how we learn and interact [1]. Virtual reality immerses viewers in a virtual environment while augmented reality overlays digital visuals on real-world objects. They connect virtual and real worlds together using enhanced 3D visuals, simulation, etc., and offer an enriched user experience to the user.

The legal profession has historically been perceived as somewhat traditional, with a strong reliance on physical documents, courtrooms, and face-to-face interactions. It stands at the crossroads of tradition and innovation, where centuries-old principles of justice meet cutting-edge technology. Virtual reality (VR) technology has emerged as a transformative force in various industries, offering immersive and interactive experiences that transport users into simulated environments. Companies increasingly recognize the power of immersive technologies to transform the business environment. Over the past few years, VR has been quietly making inroads into the legal field. The intersection of law and VR offers unique opportunities, especially for those who are tech-savvy and open to exploring non-traditional career paths. In the legal field, the applications of virtual reality have been gaining momentum, particularly in the realm of legal demonstrations.

From virtual reality (VR) and augmented reality (AR) to mixed reality (MR) and extended reality (XR), immersive technologies are tools by which computer-aided stimuli create the immersive illusion of being somewhere else. They are tools a law firm can use to assist their broader purpose of serving clients. They have the potential to completely transform how legal professionals manage cases. The immersive technologies are not only changing the way people interact with digital environments but also how legal professionals approach their work [2].

The purpose of this chapter is to explore the impact of immersive technologies on law practice. The chapter begins with explaining what immersive technologies are. It discusses immersive technologies in law and their applications. It highlights the benefits and challenges of immersive technologies in law. The last section concludes with comments.

6.2 WHAT ARE IMMERSIVE TECHNOLOGIES?

The first step in understanding how to use immersive technologies is to learn the differences between its various forms. In their simplest form, immersive technologies consist in adding virtual objects to the real world. There are four types of digital realities leading to different types of immersive technologies [3,4]:

- *Augmented reality* (AR)— designed to add digital elements over real-world views with limited interaction.

- *Virtual reality* (VR)— immersive experiences helping to

isolate users from the real world, usually via a headset device and headphones designed for such activities.

- *Mixed reality* (MR)— combining AR and VR elements so that digital objects can interact with the real world means businesses can design elements anchored within a real environment.

- *Extended reality* (XR)— covering all types of technologies that enhance our senses, including the three types previously mentioned.

These devices also enable new user interactions including spatially tracked 3D controllers, voice inputs, gaze tracking, and hand gesture controls.

Extended reality (XR) is the overarching term used to describe employing technology to blend real life and the digital world. It includes all the machine-human interfaces beyond the physical realm (reality) such as augmented reality (AR), mixed reality (MR), assisted reality (aR), and virtual reality (VR), as illustrated in Figure 6.1 [5]. Figure 6.2 shows the XR spectrum [6].

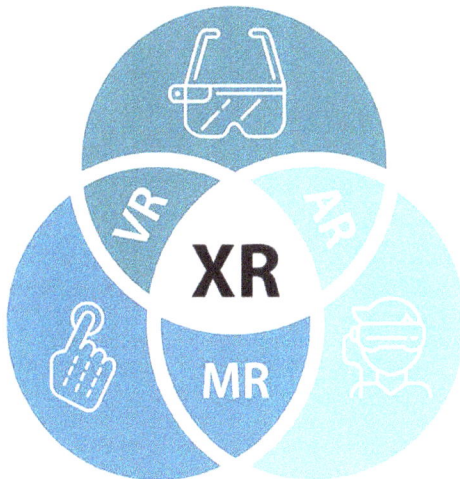

Figure 6.1 Extended reality (XR) includes AR,MR, and VR [5].

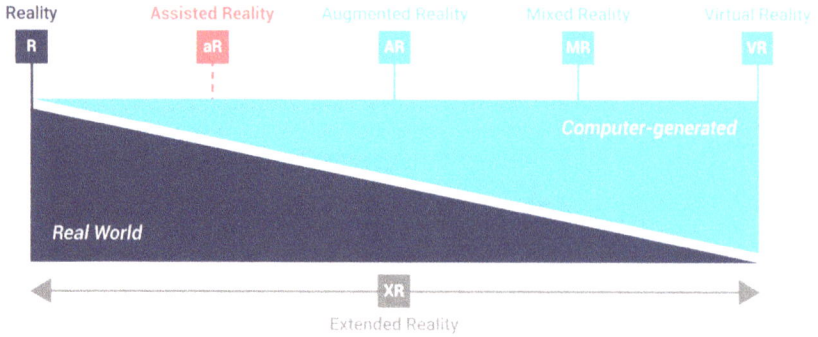

Figure 6.2 The XR spectrum [6].

Immersive technologies reside along a continuous scale ranging between the completely real and the completely virtual world. At one end, the real environment refers to the actual physical space, objects, and people that exist in the tangible world around us. At the other end, the virtual environment represents a completely computer-generated and immersive digital space, distinct from the physical reality. The space in the middle is called mixed reality, which is a blend of the real and virtual environments, where digital and physical elements coexist and interact in real time. A range of devices makes up XR, and these are used by consumers and in many industries for entertainment, safety, training, or productivity purposes.

1. *VIRTUAL REALITY:* Virtual reality (VR) is XR at its most extreme. It completely immerses the user in a digital world, often using a computer-generated environment with scenes and objects that appear to be real. The term "virtual reality" essentially means "near-reality." Virtual reality is the key technology for experiencing sensations of sight, hearing, and touch of the past, present, and future. VR is a fully immersive technology where users wear a head-mounted display and experience a simulated world of imagery and sounds. VR enables active learning. The terms, "virtual reality" and "cyberspace" are often used interchangeably. A cyberspace may be regarded as a networked virtual reality. A person using virtual reality can look around an artificial world, move around it, and interact with virtual features or items. This effect

is commonly created by virtual reality headsets. Head-mounted displays immerse the user in a virtual environment. Virtual reality is a simulated experience that can be similar to or different from the real world. It is a computer-generated, 3D environment that completely immerses the senses of sight, sound, and touch. The complete immersion of the senses overwhelms users engrossing them in the action. Virtual reality technology includes multiple components divided into two main groups: hardware and software components [7].

- *Hardware Components:* The hardware components include a computer workstation, sensory displays, a tracking system, wearable devices, and input devices. Sensory displays are used to display the simulated virtual worlds to the user. The most common type is the head-mounted displays (HMDs), which is used in combination with tracking systems. Head-mounted displays are shown in Figure 6.3 [8].

Figure 6.3 Head-mounted displays [8].

Users interact with the simulated environment through some wearable devices. VR depends on special responses such as raising hands, turning the head, or swinging the body. A wearable device is important in making these effects realistic. Special input devices are required to interact with the virtual world. These include the 3D mouse, the wired glove, motion controllers, and optical tracking sensors. These devices are used to stimulate our senses together to create the illusion of reality.

- *Software Components:* Besides the hardware, the underlying software plays an important role. It is responsible for the managing of I/O devices and time-critical applications. The software components are 3D modeling software, 2D graphics software, digital sound editing software, and VR simulation software. VR technology has been designed to ensure visual comfort and ergonomic usage.

2. *AUGMENTED REALITY:* Augmented reality (AR) is a technology that combines real-world environments with computer-generated generated information such as images, text, videos, animations, and sound. It can record and analyze the environment in real-time. In augmented reality, the user typically experiences the real world through a device such as a smartphone, tablet, smart glasses, or head-mounted display. For example, AR allows consumers to visualize a product in more detail before they purchase it. This feature enhances consumer interaction and helps them never to repurchase the wrong item. The key objective of AR is to bring computer-generated objects into the real world and allows the user only to see them. In other words, we use AR to track the position and orientation of the user's head to enhance/ augment their perception of the world. Augmented reality falls into two categories: 2D information overlays and 3D presentations, like those used with games. AR blends the virtual and real worlds by overlaying digital objects and information onto the users' view of the physical world.

To obtain a sufficiently accurate representation of reality, AR needs the following five components [9]:

- *Sensors:* AR needs suitable sensors in the environment and possibly on a user, including fine-grained geolocation and image recognition. These are activating elements that trigger the display of virtual information.

- *Image augmentation:* This requires techniques such as image processing and face recognition.

- *Head-mounted Display:* HMDs are used to view the augmented world where the virtual computer-generated information is properly aligned with the real world. Display technologies are of two types: video display and optical see-through display.

- *User Interface:* This includes technologies for input modalities that include gaze tracking, touch, and gesture. AR is a user interface technology in which a camera-recorded view of the real world is augmented with computer-generated content such as graphics, animations, and 2D or 3D models.

- *Information infrastructure:* AR requires significant computing and communications infrastructure undergirding all these technologies. The infrastructure determines what real-world components to augment, with what, and when.

3. *MIXED REALITY:* Mixed reality (MR) is a term used to describe the merging of a real-world environment and a computer-generated one. Physical and virtual objects may co-exist in mixed reality environments and interact in real time. This is an extension of AR that allows real and virtual elements to interact in an environment. MR liberates us from screen-bound experiences by offering instinctual interactions with data in our living spaces and with our friends. Online explorers, in hundreds of millions around the world, have experienced mixed reality through their handheld devices. Mixed reality is a blend of physical and digital worlds, unlocking natural and intuitive 3D human, computer, and environmental interactions, as shown in Figure 6.4 [10].

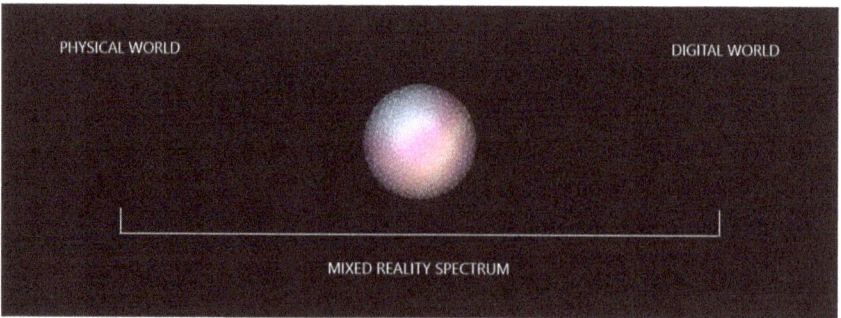

Figure 6.4 Mixed reality is a blend of physical and digital worlds [10].

This new reality is based on advancements in computer vision, graphical processing, display technologies, input systems, and cloud computing. Mixed reality has been used in applications across fields including design, education, entertainment, military training, healthcare, product content management, and human-in-the-loop operation of robots [11].

4.   *ASSISTED REALITY:* Like mixed reality, assisted reality (aR) is an extension of augmented reality, with a few notable differences to both. One of these differences is that aR is primarily hands-free through the wearing of a headset, whereas AR usually requires the holding of a device such as a mobile phone. While MR is a digital-first, real-world second reality, aR is a real-world first system. It combines software and a head-mounted display. It is best experienced using smart glasses or other wearable technology. The aR market is growing rapidly and promises to be the next great leap to boost workers' productivity. A worker wearing an aR device is shown in Figure 6.5 [12].

Figure 6.5 A worker wearing an assisted reality device [12].

5.   *EXTENDED REALITY:* The term "extended reality" (XR) has recently gained favor as an umbrella term that encompasses all of AR, VR, and MR. The primary user inputs for XR devices are described as follows. Voice interfaces are now ubiquitous thanks to mobile devices and standalone smart speakers. Apple's Siri, Amazon's Alexa, Google's Assistant, and Microsoft's Cortana are all voice-driven software interfaces that are continuously gaining new capabilities. Many XR devices enable user control with handheld controllers, which have capabilities beyond button press inputs. Both voice-driven interfaces and human-computer interactions have been developed specifically for XR devices, including gaze and gesture controls [13]. Figure 6.6 compares conventional computing with extended reality [13].

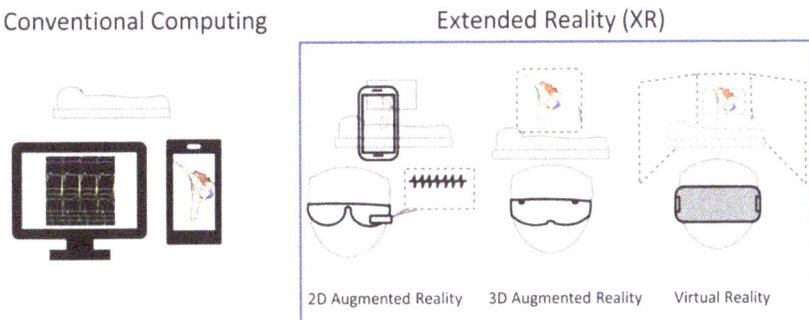

Conventional Computing   Extended Reality (XR)

2D Augmented Reality   3D Augmented Reality   Virtual Reality

Figure 6.6 Comparing conventional computing with extended reality [13].

6.3 IMMERSIVE TECHNOLOGIES IN LEGAL FIELD

Virtual reality (VR) is rapidly changing the way we perceive and interact with the world around us. Initially developed for gaming and entertainment, VR technology has found its way into various industries, including healthcare, education, and even law. VR provides a level of immersion and detail that traditional methods cannot match. Judges, juries, and legal professionals can gain a deeper understanding of complex cases by experiencing the events in a more realistic and interactive manner. As the courtroom is getting technologically advanced, VR will be able to revolutionize legal proceedings, from evidence presentation to personnel training. VR is swiftly reshaping how legal cases are tried in court. Figure 6.7 shows the use of VR in the courtroom [14], while Figure 6.8 shows some lawyers using VR [15]. Beyond the courtroom, VR serves as a valuable training tool for legal personnel.

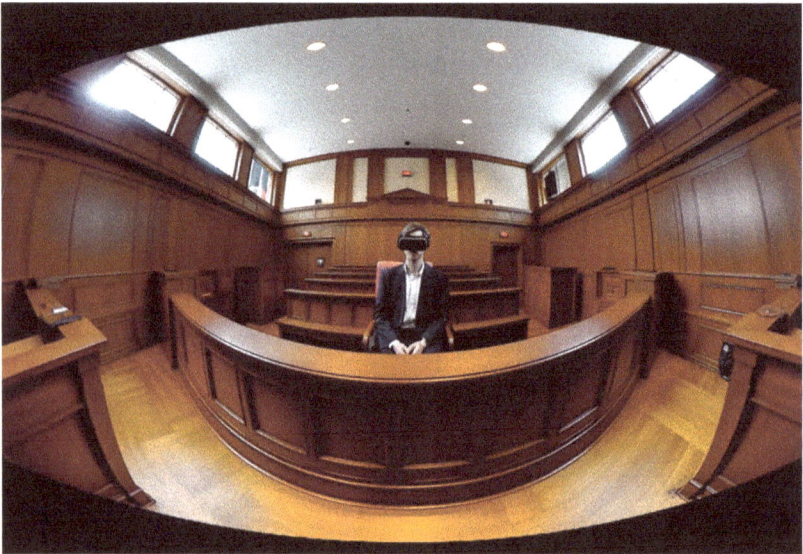

Figure 6.7 Use of VR in the courtroom [14].

Figure 6.8 Some lawyers using VR [15].

Immersive technology refers to any technology that blurs the line between the physical and digital worlds, creating a sense of presence and engagement for the user. Immersive technologies are at the forefront of innovation in the consumer technology and life sciences industries. Immersive environments increase efficiency in industry by allowing more thorough and accurate interrogation of an object or environment in real-time. The impact of VR is increasingly felt across a range of industries, and the legal sector is also one of them. As the courtroom is getting technologically advanced, VR will be able to revolutionize legal proceedings, from evidence presentation to personnel training [16].

6.4 APPLICATIONS OF IMMERSIVE TECHNOLOGIES IN LAW

The potential applications of immersive technology are vast and diverse. Initially, VR was primarily used for training purposes, such as creating immersive courtroom simulations for law students to practice their trial skills. As the technology has advanced and become more accessible, its applications in law have expanded to include litigation, mediation, client interactions, legal documentation, legal education, legal research, legal simulation, and client consultations. We now elaborate on specific applications of immersive technology in the law field [17,18]:

• *Legal Demonstrations:* Legal demonstrations are an integral part of the legal process. They involve presenting evidence, recreating scenarios, or providing visual aids to help judges, juries, and legal professionals better understand complex cases. Traditionally, these demonstrations relied on physical exhibits, photographs, diagrams, and witness testimonies. One of the most impactful applications of VR in legal demonstrations is crime scene reconstruction. VR technology can recreate the crime scene in a 3D virtual environment, enabling legal professionals, judges, and juries to walk through the scene as if they were physically present. In personal injury cases or disputes involving vehicular accidents, VR can be a game-changer. The integration of virtual reality into legal demonstrations offers a wide range of benefits, both for legal professionals and the justice system in general.

• *Property and Intellectual Property Disputes:* Virtual reality plays a pivotal role in property and intellectual property disputes. In cases involving real estate, VR can create immersive virtual tours of properties, allowing parties to examine every detail without the need for physical visits. For intellectual property disputes, VR can be used to showcase product designs, patents, trademarks, and copyrights in a visually engaging manner. Instead of relying solely on documents and legal arguments, VR allows stakeholders to experience the alleged infringement firsthand, leading to more compelling and persuasive presentations. Copyright issues loom large as VR content creation burgeons, raising questions about ownership and protection of intellectual property.

• *Witness Testimonies:* VR can enhance the way witness testimonies are presented and received in court. Traditional methods involve witnesses recounting events verbally or through written statements. However, human memory is fallible, and details can be overlooked or distorted over time. With VR, witnesses can provide their accounts in a more immersive and accurate manner. They can step into a virtual environment that replicates the scene of the event, helping them recall details more vividly.

• *Predictive Analytics:* This is another powerful tool that can be integrated into VR applications for legal demonstrations. By analyzing historical case data, predictive analytics can provide legal professionals with insights into potential outcomes and strategies. This can help attorneys make more informed decisions when presenting their cases and predicting how judges and juries might respond to different arguments. Predictive analytics and data analysis capabilities within VR environments will become increasingly sophisticated.

• *Legal Education:* Education is another area that stands to benefit greatly from immersive technologies. Colleges and universities are beginning to incorporate VR into legal studies, providing students with immersive learning experiences. This integration of VR in legal education is preparing future lawyers for the technological advancements they will encounter in their careers. Educators are using immersive technologies to enhance students' professional development. The use of VR in legal education will expand, providing law students with immersive learning experiences. Virtual reality can be used to simulate courtrooms, trial proceedings, and legal scenarios, allowing students to practice and refine their skills in a realistic virtual environment. Law graduates have the opportunity to offer consultancy services to VR companies, addressing a range of legal challenges.

• *Litigation:* The use of VR technology in litigation is becoming increasingly prevalent, offering law graduates a unique specialization. By recreating crime scenes or accident sites in a virtual environment, attorneys can present evidence in a more immersive and comprehensible manner. This specialization requires not only a firm grasp of legal principles but also an adeptness in storytelling and technological skills to effectively convey complex scenarios in a VR setting. By using immersive technologies, lawyers can create immersive presentations that help the judge and jury understand complex scenarios and visualize evidence in a way that was never before possible.

• *Immersive Evidence Presentation:* One of the most promising applications of AR and VR in the legal sector is through augmented reality presentations. Traditionally, attorneys have relied on static exhibits, documents, and verbal descriptions to make their cases.

For legal firms, integrating AR and VR into legal practices is set to transform how evidence is presented through augmented reality presentations, cases are prepared, and decisions are made. AR and VR allow for the creation of 3D models of crime scenes, accident reconstructions, and virtual walkthroughs. This immersive approach helps jurors and judges better understand the context and intricacies of a case. In some criminal trials, AR has been used to recreate crime scenes, allowing jurors to walk through the scene and examine evidence from multiple angles.

• *Legal Simulation:* This refers to the practice of replicating legal scenarios or situations for the purpose of education, training, or skill development. The primary goal of legal simulation is to provide law students and legal professionals with practical experience and a deeper understanding of the legal processes they will encounter in their careers. Educators have recognized the need for experiential learning, leading to the development of various legal simulation tools. These tools included moot court competitions, mock trial programs, and role-playing exercises, all designed to bridge the gap between theory and practice. Unlike traditional methods of legal simulation, which often rely on paper-based materials or computer simulations, VR offers a fully immersive and interactive experience. While creating physical simulations or conducting real trials can be costly and logistically challenging, VR offers a cost-effective and easily accessible alternative. A typical applications of VR in legal simulation is shown in Figure 6.9 [19].

Figure 6.9 A typical applications of VR in legal simulation [19].

6.5 BENEFITS

AR and VR have been the most promising technologies aimed at bringing tech-driven transformation to a variety of sectors. The combination offers various benefits and enables organizations to embark on the path of digitization. The legal sector is one of the many that can be greatly affected by the use of AR and VR. The application of VR in legal settings can revolutionize how evidence is presented, making it more accessible and understandable for juries and judges. Other benefits include the following [17,20]:

• *Enhanced Understanding:* VR provides a level of immersion and detail that traditional methods cannot match. Judges, juries, and legal professionals can gain a deeper understanding of complex cases by experiencing the events in a more realistic and interactive manner.

• *Time and Cost Savings:* VR can save both time and costs in the legal process. It eliminates the need for physical reconstructions, extensive travel, and the transportation of evidence. Virtual courtrooms and remote depositions save time and resources while maintaining the integrity of legal processes. Additionally, VR can expedite case preparation, as it enables legal professionals to access and review evidence more efficiently.

• *Persuasion:* The immersive nature of VR makes legal demonstrations more engaging and persuasive. When judges and juries are actively involved in the case through VR experiences, they are more likely to retain and appreciate the presented information. This can lead to more favorable outcomes for the parties involved.

• *Accessibility:* Immersive technologies are more accessible than ever. VR can make legal proceedings more accessible to individuals with disabilities. Virtual environments can be tailored to accommodate various accessibility needs, such as providing visual or auditory cues for those with hearing or visual impairments. This is a significant step towards a more equitable justice system.

• *Collaboration:* AR can enhance remote client meetings and create collaborative workspaces for legal teams. AR makes remote meetings more interactive and engaging, improving communication and understanding. It also allows legal teams to work together on case preparation from different locations, facilitating real-time collaboration and increasing overall efficiency.

• *Communication:* Many law firms have employed the use of AR and VR to improve client engagement and team communication. It is easier to communicate with your teams from the comfort of your home as a lawyer. Virtual reality facilitates better communication between legal professionals, witnesses, and clients. It allows for clearer presentations of evidence and arguments, reducing the risk of misinterpretation.

6.6 CHALLENGES AND CONCERNS

Immersive technologies do not come without challenges. Although their integration into legal demonstrations offers numerous advantages, it presents certain challenges and concerns. Implementing VR and AR technology can be daunting, especially if you are not familiar with the latest trends and best practices. As technologies such as augmented reality presentations are increasingly implemented in legal situations, legal challenges will inevitably arise. As with all technology implementation, the challenge is using these tools to enhance existing processes. Other challenges include the following [17,21]:

• *Costs:* Cost is a major hurdle, with VR setups costing anywhere from several thousand dollars to hundreds of thousands of dollars, potentially limiting access for smaller courts and underfunded jurisdictions. Implementing VR technology can be expensive, especially for smaller law firms or courts with limited budgets. This includes the cost of VR headsets, software development, and ongoing maintenance. However, as VR technology becomes more widespread, costs are likely to decrease over time.

• *Training:* Legal professionals and judges may require training to effectively use VR technology in court. Familiarity with VR interfaces and tools is essential to ensure that the technology enhances rather than hinders the legal process. Training programs and resources will be necessary to bridge this knowledge gap.

• *Data Security and Privacy:* Privacy concerns take center

stage in VR environments. With VR technologies collecting vast amounts of personal data, there is a heightened focus on privacy and security. Immersive technologies can collect and display real-time data, raising concerns about the privacy and security of this information. VR applications in legal demonstrations involve sensitive case-related data. Ensuring the security and privacy of this information is crucial. Legal organizations must implement robust data protection measures to safeguard against breaches or unauthorized access. Legal practitioners must navigate issues carefully to comply with privacy laws and regulations.

• *Ethical Concerns:* The use of VR in legal demonstrations raises ethical questions, such as the potential for manipulation or bias in virtual reconstructions. Could immersing judges in a virtual scene introduce emotional bias? How can we ensure these recreations are both accurate and fair? Legal professionals must adhere to ethical standards and guidelines to maintain the integrity of the justice system. As the use of VR in legal demonstrations grows, legal and ethical guidelines specific to this technology will continue to develop. Regulatory bodies and legal organizations will establish best practices to ensure the responsible and ethical use of VR in the courtroom.

• *Intellectual Property:* VR content creation presents a myriad of intellectual property (IP) challenges, necessitating vigilant attention from legal practitioners. Copyright issues loom large as VR content creation burgeons, raising questions about ownership and protection of intellectual property.

• *Regulatory Compliance:* As immersive technologies become more prominent, organizations and agencies are starting to focus on creating regulatory processes and guidance for these novel products. As immersive technology innovation continues to outpace development of existing regulatory frameworks, companies need to be diligent in their efforts to keep up with and predict best practices and regulatory questions. As VR becomes more integrated into legal education and practice, a regulatory framework is needed to ensure responsible use and adherence to ethical standards.

6.7 CONCLUSION

Immersive technology has become a buzzword in recent years, promising to revolutionize various industries and transform the way we experience the world around us. Immersive technologies, including virtual reality, augmented reality, and mixed reality, are increasingly deployed within industrial applications and are transforming the landscape of legal demonstrations. Clients, courts, businesses, opposing counsel, and the rest of the world are embracing both the benefits and the detriments of these technologies. To stay in business in the digital age, lawyers and law firms need to understand these tools because they can increase a firm's efficiency, productivity, and accuracy by orders of magnitude.

While immersive technologies in law practice are still evolving, their potential to revolutionize how lawyers interact with clients, collaborate globally, and offer more accessible legal services is significant [22]. As immersive technologies continue to advance, the legal community must adapt and embrace the opportunities that they present. The future of virtual reality in legal demonstrations is promising. Immersive technologies will become more accessible to law firms and courts of all sizes. More information on the integration of immersive technologies into the legal industry is available from the books in [23,24].

REFERENCE

[1] "Emerging legal issues in virtual reality: Exploring the intersection of law and immersive technology in 2024," March 2025,

https://www.lawcrossing.com/article/900054621/Emerging-Legal-Issues-in-Virtual-Reality-Exploring-the-Intersection-of-Law-and-Immersive-Technology/

[2] M. N. O. Sadiku, I. U. Oteniya, and J. O. Sadiku, "Immersive technologies in the legal industry," *International Journal of Trend in Scientific Research and Development, vol. 9, no. 3*, May-June 2025, pp. 473-482.

[3] M. N. O. Sadiku, C. M. M. Kotteti, and S. M. Musa, "Augmented reality: A primer," *International Journal of Trend in Research and Development, vol. 7, no. 3*, 2020.

[4] "What is augmented reality or AR?"

https://dynamics.microsoft.com/en-us/mixed-reality/guides/what-is-augmented-reality-ar/

[5] L. van Heerden, "What is extended reality?" August 2021,

https://journeyapps.com/blog/what-is-extended-reality/

[6] A. Xperteye, "What is assisted reality? Here is what you need to know," March 2022,

https://blog.amaxperteye.com/what-is-assisted-reality-here-is-what-you-need-to-know

[7] M. O. Onyesolu and F. U. Eze, "Understanding virtual reality technology: Advances and applications," *Advances in Computer Science and Engineering*, March 2011, pp. 53-70.

[8] "VR rundown: What you need to know before buying a VR System for your school,"

https://vreddo.com.au/vr-rundown-what-you-need-to-know-before-buying-a-vr-system-for-your-school/

[9] M. Singh and M. P. Singh, "Augmented reality interfaces," *IEEE Internet Computing*, November/December 2013, pp. 66-70.

[10] "What is mixed reality?" January 2023,

https://learn.microsoft.com/en-us/windows/mixed-reality/discover/mixed-reality

[11] "Mixed reality," *Wikipedia*, the free encyclopedia,

https://en.wikipedia.org/wiki/Mixed_reality

[12] "What is assisted reality? Here is what you need to know," March 2022,

https://blog.amaxperteye.com/what-is-assisted-reality-here-is-what-you-need-to-know

[13] C. Andrews et al., "Extended reality in medical practice," *Current Treat Options Cardiovasc Medicine, vol. 21, no. 4*, March 2019.

[14] "Justice in 3D: Virtual reality and its impact on legal practice,"

https://swisscognitive.ch/2023/06/06/justice-in-3d-virtual-reality-and-its-impact-on-legal-practice/#:~:text=To%20summarize%2C%20Virtual%20Reality%20has,and%20dynamics%20of%20a%20case.

[15] "Exploring the future of immersive technology," July 2023,

https://www.talespin.com/reading/exploring-the-future-of-immersive-technology

[16] "In 3D: Virtual reality and its impact on legal practice,"

https://e-space.mmu.ac.uk/629103/1/Immersive%20technology%20for%20tomorrow.pdf

[17] A. Tran, "Virtual reality applications in legal demonstrations," October 2023,

https://powerpatent.com/blog/virtual-reality-applications-in-legal-demonstrations

[18] C. Wilson, "Exploring the intersection of law and virtual reality: New opportunities for law graduates,"

https://legalcareerpath.com/the-intersection-of-law-and-virtual-reality/

[19] A. Tran, "Role of virtual reality in legal simulation," October 2023,

https://powerpatent.com/blog/role-of-virtual-reality-in-legal-simulation

[20] K. Panchal, "AR and VR: Modernizing the legal sector in 9 ways," November 2022,

https://www.ifourtechnolab.com/blog/ar-and-vr-modernizing-the-legal-sector-in-9-ways

[21] "Immersive technologies: The uncertain regulatory landscape," August 2024,

https://www.mofo.com/resources/insights/240830-immersive-technologies-the-uncertain-regulatory-landscape

[22] F. Mundin, "Immersive justice: Exploring the future of law practice through virtual reality," September 2023,

https://www.lawcrossing.com/article/900054992/Immersive-Justice-Exploring-the-Future-of-Law-Practice-Through-Virtual-Reality/

[23] M. C. Dieck, S. M. C. Loureiro, and T. H. Jung, *Augmented Reality and Virtual Reality: New Trends in Immersive Technology*. Springer, 2021.

[24] S. Aurelia, *Immersive Technologies: Navigating the Impacts, Challenges, and Opportunities*. Boca Raton, FL: CRC Press, 2024.

CHAPTER 7
BLOCKCHAIN IN LAW PRACTICE

*"The whole point of using a blockchain is to let people —
in particular, people who don't trust one another — share
valuable data in a secure, tamperproof way."*

—MIT Technology Review

7.1 INTRODUCTION

Historically, the legal profession is constantly playing "catch up" to technology. There is little doubt that most law firms and legal departments are burdened by massive amounts of paperwork. Lawyers are often buried in the proverbial mountain of paperwork and the classic film about the legal profession is "The Paper Chase," which ends with papers being blown all over the campus quad. Integrating the legal industry with blockchain technology will offer a higher level of precision. Known for its ability to store information in a transparent and fixed ledger, blockchain offers law firms a higher level of precision. 7.1 shows a representation of legal profession [1].

Figure 7.1 Representation of legal profession [1].

At its simplest, blockchain involves recording information in a way that creates trust in the information recorded. Blockchain is considered disruptive because it is transparent and eliminates the need for intermediaries and other third parties while being safe. Law firms should have a big picture view of how their services and practices could expand with the use of technology tools such as blockchain. As blockchain continues to advance and offer greater potential to leg professionals and firms, understanding this tech tool and leveraging its capabilities will keep legal practices at the forefront of technology [2].

Blockchain is a distributed ledger system for recording and storing transactions. At its core, blockchain is a digital ledger that records transactions across multiple computers in a way that supports the security and integrity of the data. Blockchain offers a technique to create and maintain an immutable and transparent distributed and shared ledger to be able to store information in. The legal industry is revolutionizing its operations with the help of blockchain technology. Blockchain's transparent, immutable, and secure nature allows lawyers to record and solve different types of legal matters [3].

The objective of this chapter is to explore the integration of blockchain into the legal profession. The chapter begins with explaining blockchain. It discusses blockchain in the legal industry and its applications. It highlights the benefits and challenges of blockchain in the legal industry. The last section concludes with comments.

7.2 WHAT IS BLOCKCHAIN?

Blockchain, a type of distributed digital ledger technology (DLT), is a relatively new and exciting way of recording transactions in the digital age. It is a decentralized and distributed digital ledger technology that securely records and verifies transactions across multiple computers or nodes in a network. Basically, it is a chain of blocks in which each block contains a list of transactions. The symbol of a blockchain is depicted in Figure 7.2 [4]

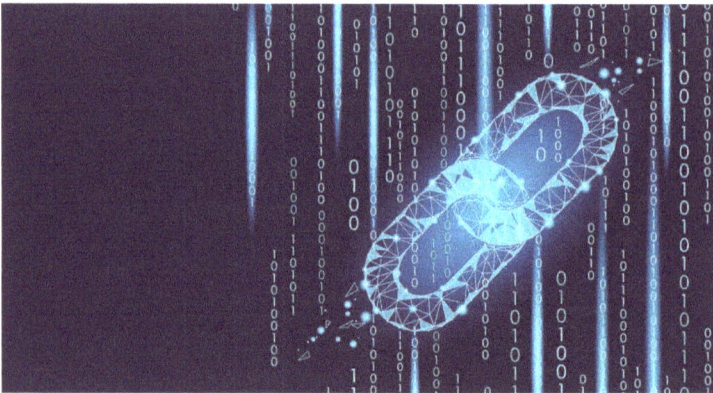

Figure 7.2 The symbol of blockchain [4].

The blockchain technology was created as the foundational basis for Bitcoin – a digital currency in which secure peer-to-peer transactions occur over the Internet. It is expected that the spending on blockchain solutions worldwide would grow from 4.5 billion USD (2020) to an estimated value of 19 billion USD by 2024 [5].

Originally developed as the accounting method for the virtual currency Bitcoin, Blockchains are appearing in a variety of commercial applications today. Blockchain technology is a type of distributed digital ledger that uses encryption to make entries permanent and tamper-proof and can be programmed to record financial transactions. It is used for secure transfer of money, assets, and information via a computer network such as the Internet without requiring a third-party intermediary. It is now being adopted across financial and non-financial sectors. As a catalyst for change, the Blockchain technology is going to change the business world and financial matters in major ways.

The first Blockchain was conceived in 2008 by an anonymous person or group known as Satoshi Nakamoto, who published a white paper introducing the concept of a peer-to-peer electronic cash system he called Bitcoin [6,7]. Bitcoin and Ethereum are the first two mainstream blockchains. Other modern blockchains include Namecoin, Peercoin, Ether, and Litecoin. Figure 7.3 shows features of blockchain [8].

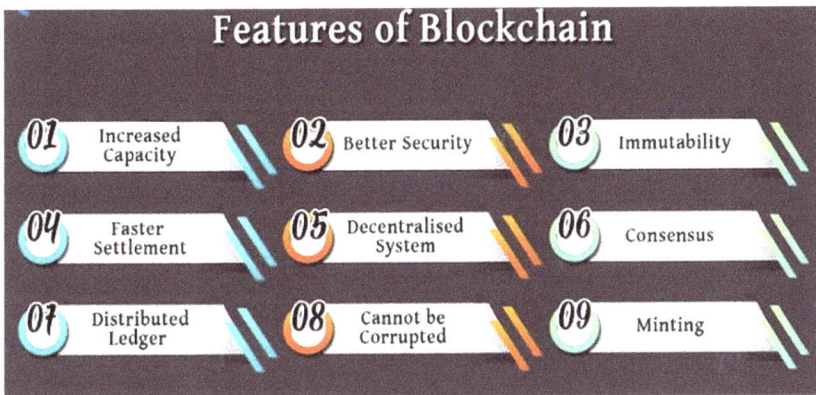

Figure 7.3 Feature of blockchain [8].

Blockchain combines existing technologies such as distributed digital ledgers, encryption, immutable records management, asset tokenization and decentralized governance to capture and record information that participants in a network need to interact and transact. As illustrated in Figure 7.4, a complete blockchain incorporates all the following five elements [9].

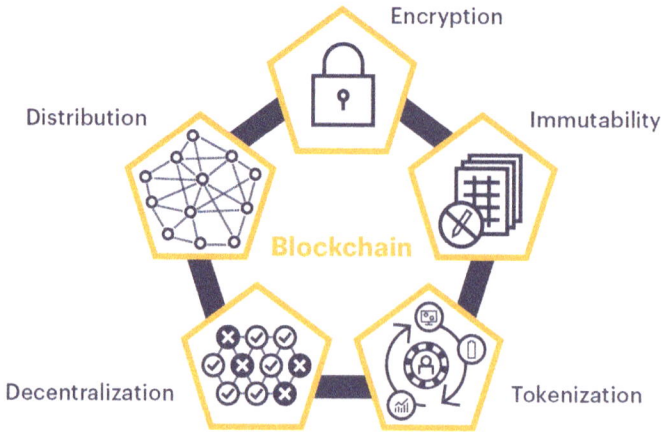

Figure 7.4 Five key elements of Blockchain [9].

- *Distribution:* Digital assets are distributed, not copied or transferred. A protocol establishes a set of rules in the form of distributed mathematical computations that ensures the integrity of the data exchanged among a large number of computing devises without going though a trusted third party. A centralized architecture presents several issues including a single point of failure and problems of scalability.

- *Encryption:* BC uses technologies such as public and private keys to record data securely and semi-anonymously. Completed transactions are cryptographically signed, time-stamped, and sequentially added to the ledger.

- *Immutability:* The blockchain was designed so these transactions are immutable, i.e. they cannot be deleted. No entity can modify the transaction records. Thus, Blockchains are secure and meddle-free by design. Data can be distributed, but not copied.

- *Tokenization:* Value is exchanged in the form of tokens, which can represent a wide variety of asset types, including monetary assets, units of data or user identities.

- *Decentralization:* No single entity controls a majority of the nodes or dictates the rules. A consensus mechanism verifies and approves transactions, eliminating the need for a central intermediary to govern the network.

Bitcoin and its underlying blockchain technology increasingly impact all facets of society. Bitcoin's status as digital gold is merely the tip of this technology. Figure 7.5 shows Bitcoin [10], while Figure 7.6 shows how blockchain works [11]. Although blockchain technology will for all time be associated with Bitcoin due to their common genesis, it has broader applications. Cryptocurrency will increasingly become a factor in family law issues as well.

Figure 7.5 Bitcoin [10].

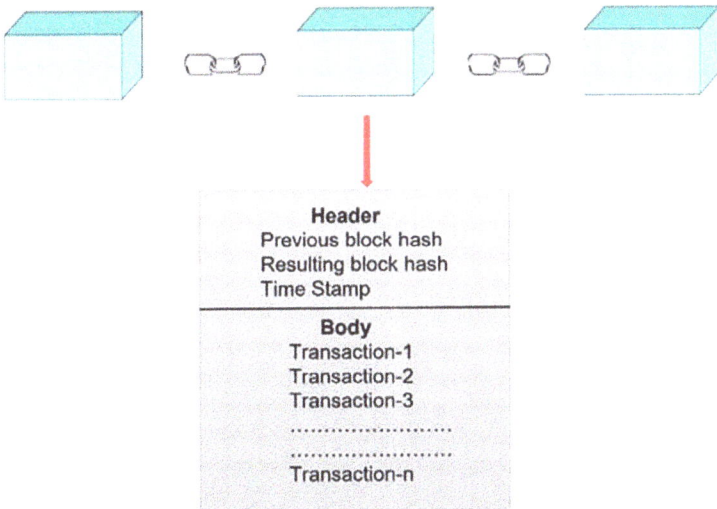

Header
Previous block hash
Resulting block hash
Time Stamp

Body
Transaction-1
Transaction-2
Transaction-3
....
....
Transaction-n

Figure 7.6 How blockchain works [11].

A blockchain is a tamper-proof, distributed database that stores blocks of information for cryptographically bound transactions via peer-to-peer networks. At the heart of blockchain's functionality is cryptographic hashing. Each block in a blockchain contains a cryptographic hash of the previous block, creating an immutable chain of blocks. If anyone attempts to tamper with the data in a block, it would alter the block's hash. This would disrupt the entire chain, making it virtually impossible to manipulate. The security feature ensures data integrity and prevents unauthorized changes [12].

In a nutshell, blockchain technology involves three basic concepts [13]: (1) It is a system for recording a series of data items (such as transactions between parties); (2) It uses cryptography to make it difficult to tamper with past entries; (3) It has an agreed process for storing copies of the ledger and adding new entries (also called a consensus protocol).

Blockchain is a novel decentralized infrastructure and distributed computing paradigm that uses a chained data structure for verification, storage, and distributed consensus algorithms to generate and update data. Decentralization is a key feature of blockchain technology, which refers to the distribution of power and decision-making across a network of nodes or participants rather than being controlled by a central authority or system. It provides robustness while eliminating many-to-one traffic flows to avoid delays and single points of failure. The advantages of decentralized property of blockchain network include the following [11]:

- The decentralized property of blockchain makes it less prone to failure and more expensive for hackers to attack the network.

- There is no third-party involvement; therefore, there is no added risk.

- Every change made in the network is traceable and concrete.

- Users maintain full autonomy of their properties and are

not dependent on third parties to maintain and manage their assets.

- It provides enhanced security.

Figure 7.7 shows different applications of blockchain [12].

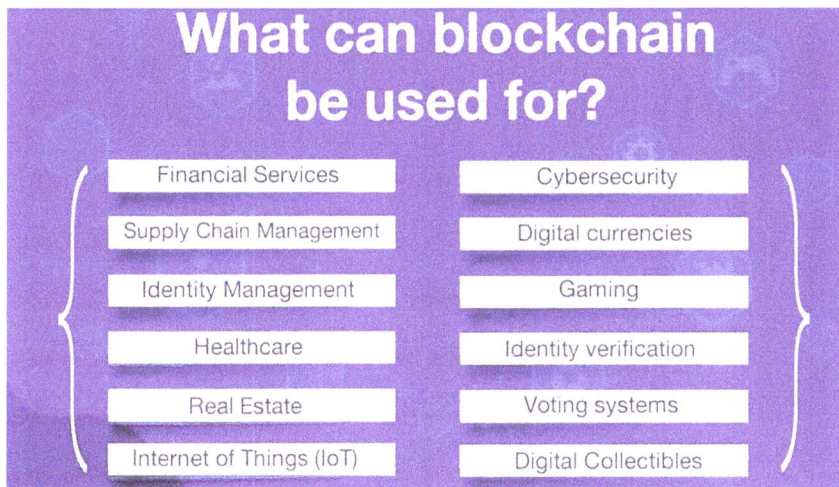

Figure 7.7 Different applications of blockchain [12].

7.3 BLOCKCHAIN IN LEGAL INDUSTRY

The legal industry has been slow to modernize. In today's digital era, the legal industry is witnessing a fundamental upheaval due to the groundbreaking technology known as blockchain. Blockchain is a comprehensive, up-to-date (real-time) ledger of anything that can be recorded from financial transactions to ownership of physical assets stored in a distributed, peer-to-peer fashion. It is essentially a repository of digital records which are cryptically stored using a cryptographic hash. Blockchain technology is changing the legal field. Blockchain is attractive because the transparent record it provides enables parties to complete transactions without a trusted authority. Blockchain-based solutions help maintain uniformity, consistency, and accuracy of data, minimize manual intervention into systems and human errors, and make sure compliance is achieved. Blockchain technology transforms how we keep and move money and redefines how legal practitioners maintain and validate vital papers and transactions. It is transforming the legal sector by offering a secure, transparent, and efficient platform for organizing and validating legal documents [13]. Figure 7.8 represents the integration of blockchain in the legal industry [14].

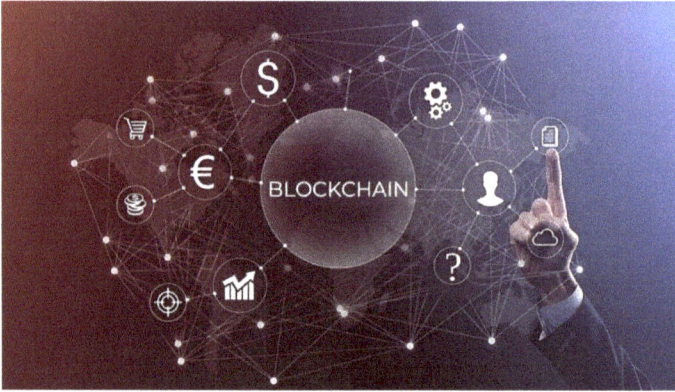

Figure 7.8 Representation of blockchain in the legal industry [14].

The legal industry, which is among the oldest and most complex industries, demands a thorough comprehension and assimilation of the law. The use of blockchain technology could potentially revolutionize the legal industry by providing a secure, transparent, and immutable ledger. It could help to reduce the risk of data being hacked or altered and could help to speed up the transaction process. Blockchain is a technology that can be used to create a secure, tamper-proof record of transactions or documents. It does this by using a distributed database that is shared by all of the users of the blockchain network. It assists lawyers in streamlining transactional processes and securely storing legal papers with electronic signatures. Lawyers see blockchain as a game-changer technology, mainly because of its unparalleled security and transparency. This technology has the potential to make legal processes more efficient, cost-effective, and reliable [15]. Its adoption in legal practices empowers professionals to navigate complexities efficiently.

7.4 APPLICATIONS OF BLOCKCHAIN IN THE LEGAL INDUSTRY

Blockchain is a remarkable technology that redefines the legal profession while providing excellent security. It has the potential to be used in a number of different ways in the legal industry. It can be applied in many different ways to make the legal system more efficient. Popular applications of blockchain in legal sectors include smart contracts, litigation and settlement, financial transactions, criminal cases, chain of custody, notary services, estate planning, and more. Specific applications of blockchain in law include the following [16,17]:

• *Smart Contracts:* Smart contracts are one of the most recognized use cases for blockchain in the legal industry. These are digitally created, and always verifiable since they are on the blockchain. Say goodbye to the manual process of contract execution. Smart contracts are the blockchain's version of what traditional contracts should be. Smart contracts are powered by blockchain technology and automatically apply conditions and terms, removing the necessity for intermediaries. Some suggest that smart contracts could replace traditional contracts and with it, lawyers. A smart contract is a self-executing computer program contained within a decentralized blockchain network. The key features of smart contracts are transparency, immutability, and efficiency. The blockchain holds the promise to change this into a digital process in what is being dubbed "smart contracts." These smart contracts could potentially be created and executed directly between the relevant parties, with less lawyer involvement.. Lawyers may find smart contracts useful for their own organizations. Blockchain in smart contract handling limits payment disputes, as smart contracts can be presented in funds when each contract term is fulfilled. If the contractual terms are not adhered to, the stop of services is immediately implemented. One of the debates about smart contracts revolves around whether or not they will replace lawyers.

• *Intellectual Property:* The law has struggled when it comes to protecting intellectual property in the digital age, including images, audio, and video files, as well as designs and symbols. Artists and musicians attempt to protect their work, but too often it gets used without their permission, and royalties do not get paid from audio streaming services that struggle with profitability. Blockchain technology is a natural fit for intellectual-property connoisseurs. Because blockchains create unalterable data, intellectual-property owners can establish the authenticity of ownership rights, combat counterfeiting, license property through smart contracts, and efficiently register trademarks by using blockchain technology. Blockchain technology can serve as an intellectual-property registry that catalogs and stores original works. Blockchain and smart contracts can be used in tandem to efficiently license intellectual property, allowing authors and licensees to interface directly without needing an intermediary. Because blockchain is irreversible, secure and time-stamped, it offers a prime way to provide evidence of first use and has applications for any kind of patents, copyrights, and trademarks. A critical blockchain-based innovation impacting intellectual property is non-fungible-tokens or NFTs. NFTs are units of digital data stored on the blockchain. These are cryptographic tokens that can be used to identify exclusive property on a blockchain.

• *Blockchain Law:* With blockchain technology having the potential to be used across many sectors, the law will need to adapt again, and there is already a need to have lawyers specializing in blockchain law – the new cutting-edge for digital law. Figure 7.9 shows various opportunities available in blockchain law [18].

Opportunities Available in Blockchain Law

- Consulting
- Legislative Tracking
- Policy Formulation
- Compliance
- Litigation

Figure 7.9 Opportunities available in blockchain law [18].

• *Property Rights:* These rights encompass how property is bought, sold, and rented. Go down to your local government property office, and it is easy to see how this arena is stuck in the last century, with piles of ledgers, paper deeds, and property cards all tracking property ownership. Just like IP rights, physical-property rights could also be stored digitally on a blockchain platform. Since the process for registering ownership of property differs between states and involves small localities, it is unlikely that a unified, digital, nationwide land registry will be adopted any time soon. The blockchain, with its inherent security and digital ledger function, promises to be an effective, secure, and immutable method to store the data essential for property rights, including land ownership, and the details of when it changed hands. The distribution of property rights and the existence of transaction costs impacts a society's economic activities, yet property rights and transaction cost structures are primarily based on the pre-digital era.

• *Chain of Custody:* Chain of custody is the method of managing evidence from the moment it is taken into custody until it can be used as evidence in the legal court. The chain of custody is an important legal concept which documents what happens to evidence in a criminal case. It is typically a paper trail that gets created for each piece of evidence, and must be fully maintained until this evidence gets presented in court. The blockchain is ideally suited for application in the chain of custody, particularly for the more challenging digital files. Here, blockchain tech can be applied to not only track the custody of documents, but also to store the documents themselves.

• *Notary Public:* Notaries can be used by both individuals and companies to verify documents and signatures before an official witness. Currently, notary publics are used to confirm and verify signatures on legal documents, such as deeds and contracts. Using blockchain technology, these documents can be preserved digitally as part of a digital ledger. The public and private keys can be utilized to verify the identity of the document's owner, using blockchain in legal industry as a powerful tool for traditional notaries. Since public notaries are officials in the state, blockchain is likely to replace notaries with significant and expensive changes to the institution.

• *Corporate Filings:* Corporate filings and other records may soon be maintained on blockchain platforms. It is possible to have every corporate document and transaction recorded on a blockchain so that there is an immutable record of all corporate acts. Governments may eventually provide blockchain platforms for companies to submit their corporate registrations and documents. Corporate lawyers may need to learn about blockchain technology to advise their clients on the logistics, benefits, and risks of corporate record keeping through blockchain.

• *Criminal Cases:* The criminal justice system stands to benefit from blockchain. Criminal cases involve voluminous documents and records, all of which must be authenticated, recorded, and stored securely. The potential of blockchain technology to revolutionize the criminal justice system is significant. This intricate and document-intensive sector is ripe for modernization. By leveraging blockchain, records can be seamlessly shared among stakeholders, from police officers to parole boards. As the case proceeds through the judicial system, each participant updates the single blockchain record with their actions, for example, the initial arrest record, indictment, and plea. These blockchain-based records can be shared with defense counsel, government attorneys, law-enforcement officers, parole officers, the court, and even victims or witnesses when appropriate. Changes show instantly and to all relevant parties.

• *Proof of Service:* Lawyers have traditionally relied on process servers to deliver court documents. While most process servers are honest and trustworthy individuals, a few are not. Blockchain may make service abuse impossible. Hypothetically, blockchain technology could provide courts, lawyers, and parties access to verifiable, tamper-proof information about service of process. Ultimately, it is conceivable for blockchain technology to eliminate human proof and manual delivery of service.

• *Blockchain-Based Arbitration:* Commercial arbitration is the preferred choice of major economic players because of being time-effective, neutral. and having high level of confidentiality. Blockchain is now being incorporated into many forms of alternative dispute resolution, particularly arbitration. In the twentieth century, arbitration became a popular method for businesses to resolve disputes without engaging in litigation. Arbitration promised to be a faster, easier process that would permit the parties to select expert adjudicators in their field rather than trusting the luck of the draw for a general civil judge or jury to resolve their dispute. Blockchain-based arbitration could offer enhanced confidentiality. It could also pave the way for automated dispute resolution, especially in the context of smart contracts. In a blockchain-based arbitration system, users write their agreements into an electronic smart contract that manages the arbitration process. These agreements are seamlessly integrated with smart contract codes to guarantee the legality of any arbitral award.

• *E-Discovery:* Legal proceedings usually contain digital evidence, ranging from electronic documents and emails to metadata from social media and other content. The digital revolution has resulted in electronic discovery (e-discovery) becoming an integral part of contemporary litigation. Blockchain application in legal industry is an amazing technological advancement poised to transform the way we deal with e-Discovery in the field of digital evidence. Whether in the form of smart contracts, blockchain-based record keeping, supply-chain management, or licensing, the mere fact that clients are using this technology means that, once a dispute arises, blockchain-based information will become discoverable as electronically stored information. Lawyers must be prepared for this possibility by developing their understanding of blockchain-based data storage and designing protocols for handling this data. Although data stored on a blockchain is reliable, it must be transferred from the blockchain to make it accessible and usable as evidence. Parties will therefore need to authenticate how they are providing blockchain-based data in discovery. Lawyers should also stay updated on how courts handle future blockchain e-discovery issues, as these decisions will provide critical guidance on clients' duties in terms of their blockchain data. Since everything is based on hard evidence, all digitally digitized evidence can be safely stored on blockchain vaults and networks.

• *Electronic Signatures:* Digitally signed documents improve the speed of processing transactions by not having to wait for client signatures. Electronic signatures bring speed, efficiency, and cost savings to the authentication process. Signing on blockchain costs the signer a fraction of the cost compared to e-signature platforms like DocuSign. Electronic signatures stored on the Ethereum blockchain live independently of the object being signed, which allows for parallel signing and independent verification without granting full read access to the content. When two parties digitally sign a smart contract, they simultaneously agree to the terms and conditions associated with the agreement.

• *Financial Transactions:* Blockchain adds transparency in the financial-services industry. By performing transactions on a public ledger, inefficiencies and fraud are easier to detect and address. One primary concern with digital transactions is the risk of hacking or scams. Blockchain technology can increase the security of transactions.

• *Tokenization:* This is another of the use cases of blockchain in legal sector. It is a technique that converts rights into assets into digital tokens. Blockchain enables the tokenization of assets. You can represent ownership of assets digitally through tokens, facilitating fractional ownership and easier transferability. The parties interested can issue tokens through a platform that supports smart contracts that allow the sale and purchase of the token through exchanges. For example, artists could tokenize and record the work on an open Ethereum blockchain, build an authorization around it, and then program real-time royalty payments.

• *Jury Trials:* One of the main use cases for blockchain in legal industry for jury trials lies in its capacity to spot patterns and relationships in the evidence. Blockchain have been used to aid lawyers in jury trials. Utilizing the natural processing of languages and machine-learning algorithms, these systems can find relevant information in transcripts, documents, audio recordings, transcripts, and video footage.

• *Document Management:* One of the most famous applications of blockchain in the legal business is in legal document management. Traditionally, legal documents such as contracts, deeds, and wills were saved and handled using paper-based methods or centralized digital databases, which were prone to mistakes, fraud, and unauthorized revisions. Blockchain systems for legal document management typically contain capabilities like as smart contracts, which are self-executing agreements with the contents of the agreement explicitly put into code. With blockchain technology, legal practitioners now have access to a safe and transparent platform for organizing and certifying essential documents. Each document is encrypted and saved on the blockchain, guaranteeing that it cannot be edited or modified without leaving a trail.

• *Estate Planning and Wills:* Traditionally, the real estate industry has grappled with issues related to land registries and property deeds. Inaccuracies in land titles, fraudulent claims, and extended transaction times have long been challenged. According to the World Bank, over 70% of the world's population lacks access to proper land titling, leading to disputes and uncertainties. The integration of blockchain into real estate offering solutions to these age-old problems. With its decentralized and immutable nature, blockchain promises to revolutionize the way land registries and property deeds are managed.

Some of these applications are portrayed in Figure 7.10 [18].

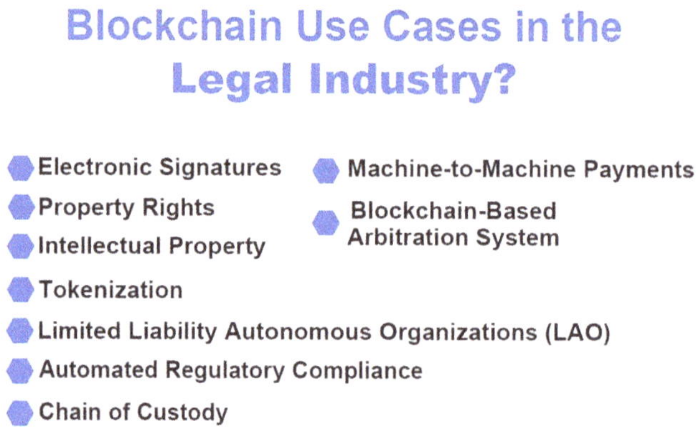

Blockchain Use Cases in the Legal Industry?

- Electronic Signatures
- Property Rights
- Intellectual Property
- Tokenization
- Limited Liability Autonomous Organizations (LAO)
- Automated Regulatory Compliance
- Chain of Custody
- Machine-to-Machine Payments
- Blockchain-Based Arbitration System

Figure 7.10 Applications of blockchain in the legal industry [18].

7.5 BENEFITS

The benefits of blockchain in law and for lawyers are numerous. Blockchain technology is more secure than our current technology and should reduce the risk of breaches. It could revolutionize the legal field by providing automation, increased security, operational efficiency, better transparency, global accessibility, and cost savings. It can help to reduce the risk of fraud and corruption and allows for the secure and transparent sharing of information. Other benefits of blockchain in law include the following [19]:

• *Automation:* Integrating blockchain automates various legal processes. This automation minimizes error risks and saves time in repetitive legal procedures. Lawyers spend up to 48% of their time on administrative tasks, including transferring information between software and updating client trust ledgers. Utilizing a legal agreement repository and pre-fabricated smart contracts, lawyers can automate non-billable administrative tasks and transactional work. One of the more well-known applications of blockchain in legal industry is document management. In the past, legal documents such as deeds, contracts, and wills were kept and processed using paper or central digital databases, prone to errors, fraud, and unauthorized revisions. With blockchain technology, lawyers can now access an efficient and secure platform to organize and verify crucial documents.

- *Regulatory Compliance:* Today, legal professionals are facing multiple challenges related to regulatory compliance management and globalization. Research has shown that blockchain technologies can improve regulatory compliance and regulators as a whole. Blockchain application in legal sector provides us with the foundation to build an open ledger system in which diverse parties can timely report their compliance data or documents to the authorities of their choice.

- *Data Security:* One of the major advantages of blockchain in legal industry is its ability to offer secure, tamper-proof document storage. Legal records, often targeted by malevolent cyber attackers, stand protected with blockchain's decentralized architecture. With blockchain technology, delicate legal documents are stored in decentralized systems, so they cannot be altered or compromised. Lock-and-key and username-password protective measures do not necessarily keep the files tamper-proof

- *Cost Efficiency:* Elimination of manual work means automatic reduction of costs. By removing the need for middlemen and lowering the possibility of mistakes and conflicts, blockchain technology may lead to cost savings for legal practitioners and their clients. AI automation can reduce the requirement for manual tasks such as document drafting, reviewing, filing, and review. This reduces time and lowers the operational cost for law firms. Due to AI's accuracy and speed, things that were once time-consuming can now be accomplished in just a few minutes.

- *Operational Efficiency:* The adoption of blockchain not only digitizes but enhances myriad legal operations without undermining judicial sanctity. By redefining both crucial and administrative tasks, it curtails unnecessary overheads and frictions.

- *Legal Research:* Traditional legal research is lengthy and labor-intensive. AI-powered tools enable lawyers to study huge collections of legislation, case law, and precedents for law in just a fraction of the time. These tools deliver quicker, more precise outcomes, allowing legal professionals to concentrate on more strategic projects.

• *Accessibility:* Each AI and blockchain enable lawyers and their users to collaborate from anywhere around the globe. Legal documents are signed electronically, and research conducted via the Internet is undertaken via blockchain smart contracts. Without the need for physical meetings or manually drafted paperwork, blockchain smart contracts may be implemented globally.

• *Dispute Resolution:* Blockchain is a revolutionary technology for dispute resolution. It provides precise and tamper-proof records of all communications and transactions. This transparency makes mediation and arbitration procedures quicker and fair.

• *Reduction in Legal Fees:* The use of blockchain enables lawyers to streamline their transactional work, digitally sign documents, and immutably store legal agreements. As a result, scripted text and automated contract management reduce the time spent preparing documents, sorting files and organizing paperwork. There are huge cost savings here as the cost of physically storing these documents is eliminated, and clients no longer have to pay for the excessive time lawyers spend preparing these documents.

• *Transparency:* The transparent nature of blockchain means that all parties participating in a legal transaction have access to the same information, eliminating the chance of disputes and misunderstandings. Moreover, contracts created through blockchain have additional built-in compliance, which reduces risk and any chance of misinterpretation. Additionally, due to the highly secure nature of blockchain, it is easy to access the chain of custody with digital documents.

• *Collaboration:* Blockchain fosters efficient collaboration among legal entities. By sharing a decentralized ledger, multiple parties involved in a legal matter can access, update, and verify information in real-time. This accessibility enhances collaboration and speeds up decision-making processes.

• *Data Integrity:* Blockchain ensures data integrity through its immutable nature. Legal records remain tamper-proof, maintaining their credibility. Data is not manipulated, malicious or misinterpreted as blockchain is immutable and cannot be attacked by hackers.

Some of these benefits are shown in Figure 7.11 [20].

Figure 7.11 Some benefits of blockchain in the legal industry [20].

7.6 CHALLENGES

For legal professionals, there are a few of the challenges to be overcome in adopting blockchain. The potential challenges of using blockchain in the Legal industry include the lack of regulation, regulatory hurdles, scalability issues, as well as education and training. As blockchain is a relatively new technology, there is some uncertainty around its legality and how it should be used. Other challenges of blockchain in law include the following [19]:

- *Data Privacy and Security:* Maintaining data privacy and security poses significant challenges. Blockchain's transparent nature conflicts with data privacy laws, requiring innovative solutions to safeguard sensitive information while maintaining transparency.

- *Data Protection:* Another legal issue faced by blockchain software development companies is protecting their data. Due to the decentralization provided by blockchain technologies, it may be difficult to monitor how personal information can be collected, utilized, and stored.

- *Fraud Prevention:* Fraud has become a serious problem for both individuals and businesses. It is any deliberate fraud or deceit carried out to gain an unfair advantage or inflict damage. Fraudulent activities could result in significant loss of money, damage to reputation, and loss of trust.

- *Regulatory Uncertainty:* The legal profession being already extremely risk-averse alongside the uncertainty regarding the regulation of blockchain technologies makes blockchain adoption a big challenge for law firms. Uncertainty in regulatory compliance is a significant legal hurdle facing blockchain-based startups. Because of blockchain technologies' decentralization, it is sometimes difficult to identify the laws and regulations that apply to a specific project.

- *Intellectual Property:* Another issue in the legal world for blockchain-based startups is protecting intellectual property (IP). Because blockchain is a global industry, it could be challenging to apply IP rights across many countries. This is a significant issue for startups seeking to safeguard their software.

- *Taxation:* Another legal issue faced by blockchain startups is the tax burden. Because blockchain is a global sector, it is often difficult to know which tax laws apply to a specific venture. Knowing the tax consequences of your blockchain project is essential to its success.

- *Scalability:* This has been cited as a reason blockchains cannot be used in the legal industry, although as blockchain technology develops, this is becoming less of an issue.

- *Cybersecurity:* The legal industry continues to be a major focus for cybercriminals, and the leading cybersecurity solutions providers continue to develop innovative products to solve two significant problems: data loss and data leaks in the cloud. Hackers are aggressively targeting law firms' data because they have access to their clients' most valuable information. Law firms need to implement exceptionally secure mechanisms to protect content and file sharing to ensure that only authorized partners can access highly confidential documents, including data encryption capabilities or file-level usage rights.

- *Complex Technology:* The intricacies of blockchain technology pose challenges for legal professionals. It requires specialized knowledge to understand its technical aspects and apply legal principles to this complex system.

7.7 CONCLUSION

By offering a decentralized and secure method of recording transactions, blockchain is fundamentally transforming how legal transactions are handled. Blockchain is not going away anytime soon, as it continues to become a transformative force for lawyers. The emergence of this technology has led to an increased role for lawyers in different areas, opening more doors for legal professionals to explore. Entering the blockchain industry as a lawyer presents an exciting array of opportunities. Figure 7.12 provides some reasons lawyers should join the blockchain industry [12].

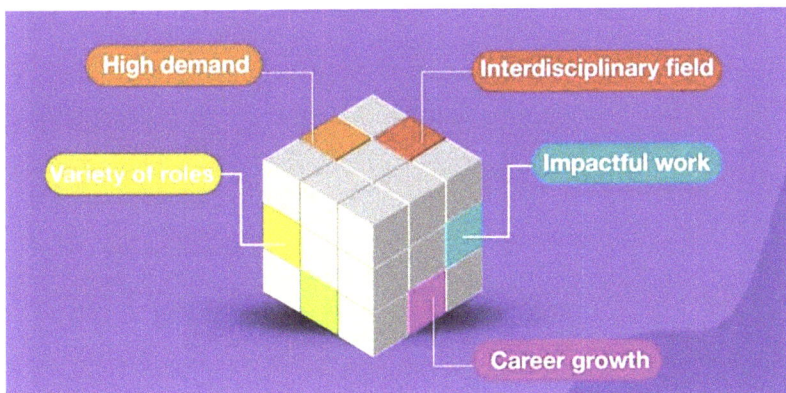

Figure 7.12 Why lawyers should join the blockchain industry [12].

Blockchain technology has the potential to revolutionize many industries, and blockchain lawyers are in a unique position to help clients navigate the legal implications of this new technology. The impact of blockchain technology on the legal industry is increasing.

The question of how and in what ways technology can be integrated seamlessly into the practice of law remains a principal concern for stakeholders involved. In the foreseeable future, blockchain may change how law firms conduct a multitude of services. More information on the integration of blockchain technology into the legal industry is available from the books in [21-31] and a related journal: *IEEE Blockchain.*

REFERENCE

[1] S. Chain, "Blockchain in law: Decentralizing the legal industry," July 2021,

https://simbachain.com/blog/blockchain-in-law-decentralizing-the-legal-industry/

[2] "Legal tech: How blockchain can easily transform the legal profession," October 2020,

https://www.abclegal.com/blog/legal-tech-blockchain

[3] M. N. O. Sadiku, B. Oteniya, and J. O. Sadiku, "Blockchain in law," *International Journal of Trend in Scientific Research and Development, vol. 9, no. 3*, May-June 2025, pp. 310-322.

[4] "Blockchain meets the oil & gas industry," February 2018,

https://executiveacademy.at/en/news/detail/blockchain-meets-the-oil-gas-industry/

[5] C. M. M. Kotteti and M. N. O. Sadiku, "Blockchain technology," *International Journal of Trend in Research and Development, vol. 10, no. 3*, May-June 2023, pp. 274-276.

[6] "Blockchain," *Wikipedia*, the free encyclopedia

https://en.wikipedia.org/wiki/Blockchain

[7] S. Nakamoto, "Bitcoin: A peer-to-peer electronic cash system,"

https://bitcoin.org/bitcoin.pdf

[8] P. Yagnesh, "Blockchain in the legal industry: Smart contracts and beyond," July 2024,

https://www.linkedin.com/pulse/blockchain-legal-industry-smart-contracts-beyond-yagnesh-pandya-lgkif/

[9] "The CIO's guide to blockchain,"

https://www.gartner.com/smarterwithgartner/the-cios-guide-to-blockchain#:~:text=True%20blockchain%20has%20five%20elements,%2C%20immutability%2C%20tokenization%20and%20decentralization.

[10] "Blockchain and space exploration: Is decentralized data the future of space missions?" October 2024,

https://medium.com/coinmonks/is-decentralized-data-the-future-of-space-missions-646173d1aeec

[11] B. G. Celik, Y. S. Abraham, and M. Attaran, "Unlocking blockchain in construction: A systematic review of applications and barriers," *Buildings*, vol. 14, no. 6, 2024.

[12] "What does a blockchain lawyer do?" Unknown Source.

[13] "How is blockchain used in the legal industry?" April 23, 2024

https://www.linkedin.com/pulse/how-blockchain-used-legal-industry-lawblocks-ee68e/

[14] "Blockchain technology in the legal industry,"

https://consensys.io/blockchain-use-cases/law

[15] K. Panchal, "Blockchain in the Legal sector: Redefining the business in 12 ways," November 2022,

https://www.ifourtechnolab.com/blog/blockchain-in-the-legal-sector-redefining-the-business-in-12-ways

[16] J. P. DeMuro, "7 ways blockchain will change the legal industry forever," January 2018,

https://www.techradar.com/news/7-ways-blockchain-will-change-the-legal-industry-forever

[17] "How blockchain impacts the legal profession," February 2023,

https://www.jdsupra.com/legalnews/how-blockchain-impacts-the-legal-6422930/

[18] "Blockchain for lawyers: Experience legal tech advancement," February 2025,

https://webisoft.com/articles/blockchain-for-lawyers/

[19] A. Sharma, "Blockchain in legal: Use cases, benefits and challenges," October 2024,

https://www.a3logics.com/blog/blockchain-in-legal/

[20] D. Singh, "Blockchain in legal industry: Redefining legal frameworks with decentralized solutions," September 2023, p.78.

[21] M. N. O. Sadiku, *Blockchain Technology and Its Applications*. Moldova, Europe: Lambert Academic Publishing, 2023.

[22] N. Oberheiden, A. Veneziano, and P. Strickland, *The Law Of Tomorrow: Bitcoin, Tokens, Blockchain - An Introduction For Lawyers*. Expert Court Publishing, 2022.

[23] Z. Mahmood, *Industry Use Cases on Blockchain Technology Applications in Iot and the Financial Sector*. IGI Global, 2021.

[24] S. Chugani and S. T. Gannon (eds.), *Banking [on] Blockchain: A Legal and Regulatory Primer*. ABA Book Publishing, 2024.

[25] L. Cohen, P. Desai, and D. Fisher, *Blockchain and the Legal Profession*. Globe Law and Business Limited, 2018.

[26] M. Corrales, M. Fenwick, and H. Haapio(eds.), *Legal Tech, Smart Contracts and Blockchain*. Springer, 2019.

[27] S. Amuial, J. N. Dewey, and J. Seul, *The Blockchain: A Guide for Legal and Business Professionals*. LegalWorks, 2016.

[28] M. Roussou, *Legal Issues Arising from Blockchain Technology in Maritime Trade*. LAP LAMBERT Academic Publishing, 2021.

[29] P. De Filippi and A. Wright, *Blockchain and the Law: The Rule of Code*. Harvard University Press, 2018.

[30] M. Artzt and T. Richter, *Handbook of Blockchain Law: A Guide to Understanding and Resolving the Legal Challenges of Blockchain Technology*. Wolters Kluwer, 2020.

[31] M. W. Rasmussen, S. L. Walling, and D. N. Giobbe (eds.), *Blockchain for Business Lawyers*. ABA Book Publishing, 2nd edition 2024.

CHAPTER 8
LITIGATION MANAGEMENT

*"At his best, man is the noblest of all animals; separated
from law and justice he is the worst."*

—Aristotle

8.1 INTRODUCTION

For proper management of data, the legal industry can use a litigation management system. In essence, litigation is the process by which the legal system attempts to resolve disputes. The filing of that lawsuit triggers the litigation process. The primary goal of litigation management is to ensure that legal disputes are handled in an organized, efficient, and effective manner. Its aim is to achieve the most favorable outcome for the client or organization, whether through court proceedings, settlements, or alternative dispute resolution methods, while simultaneously reducing costs and optimizing resources. Legal departments are starting to turn to dedicated litigation management systems as a holistic solution to address the number of challenges often faced in modern litigation.

Imagine having to consolidate documents for a decade old case. How many petitions filed? How many lawyers engaged? How many changing hearing dates? There is surely a need for dynamic management of litigation specifics to stay on top of hearing dates, to track and respond to notices, documenting all interactions between the parties and even the lawyers involved. Figure 8.1 shows a team of lawyers [1].

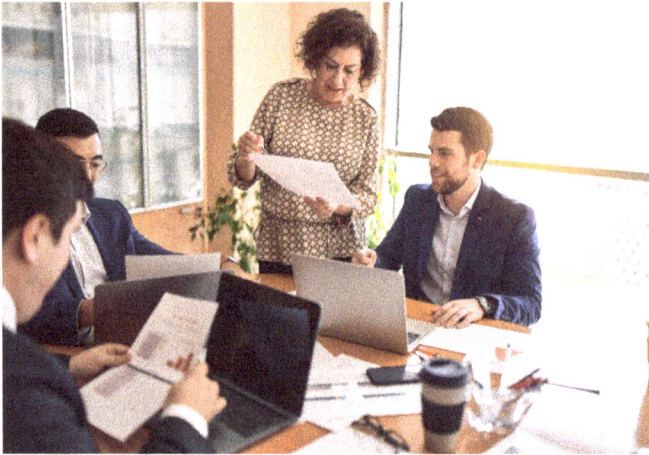

Figure 8.1 A team of lawyers [1].

Litigation management refers to the coordinated approach to overseeing and directing all phases of a lawsuit or legal dispute, from the beginning through to its resolution. At its core, litigation management is where business strategy meets legal expertise. It includes tasks such as developing legal strategies, planning budgets, coordinating with legal teams, managing documents and evidence, and facilitating communication among all involved parties. For claims organizations and risk managers seeking ways to enhance relationships with their defense attorneys through a unified platform, litigation management software makes a lot of sense [2].

This chapter is intended to be a definitive resource for litigation management. It begins with explaining the concepts of litigation and litigation management. It discusses litigation management software. It highlights the benefits and challenges of litigation management. The last section concludes with comments.

8.2 WHAT IS LITIGATION?

Litigation is simply filling a lawsuit. It is the process of filing and following through a lawsuit to enforce your rights under your insurance policy. When parties have a dispute, whether it be about a contract, personal injury, financial or family disagreement, a party may decide to file a lawsuit. Filing a lawsuit triggers a series of mechanisms that help the parties work towards resolving a dispute. While some lawsuits are resolved before a jury or a judge in court, some are settled by a out-of-court agreement between the parties involved. Many disputes or disagreements will never evolve into a traditional "lawsuit," which is why it is important to speak with an attorney as quickly as possible, to ensure that you are properly represented from the start. If the parties cannot reach an agreement on how to resolve the dispute, then a party may decide to start the litigation process or file a lawsuit [3].

Before officially filing your lawsuit, you or your public adjuster will need to provide any documents or information you have related to the property damage. Once your lawsuit is filed, the insurance company will respond to your complaints and the "discovery" phase will begin. Discovery is the process of exchanging information between the insurance company's attorney and your attorney. The last step in litigation is the trial phase. This is what most people think of when they hear the word "lawsuit," where the case goes to court before a judge and jury [4]. Throughout the litigation process, your attorney will be with you to guide you every step of the way and represent you. During the entire litigation period, your attorney and the insurance company's attorney will likely engage in negotiation techniques to avoid going to trial and continuing litigation. Every insurance claim is different and some may not require litigation at all while others may result in a lengthy litigation.

Even if a case goes to trial and ends with a verdict, that does not mean that litigation has ended. If one party is unhappy with the decision, they may choose to appeal to a higher court which may delay final resolution of the case for years. Retaining legal counsel right from the beginning is incredibly important to ensure that your case is expedited as much as is possible, and that your rights are properly represented, whether in a court of law, in private negotiations, or by mediation or arbitration.

A litigation manager is responsible for managing the litigation process of a company, including overseeing the preparation of legal documents, researching legal issues, and providing legal advice. They also work with attorneys to ensure that the company's legal interests are being properly represented in court. They must possess the ability to work under pressure and meet deadlines [1].

8.3 WHAT IS LITIGATION MANAGEMENT?

Litigation management is a focus on streamlining processes and procedures to reduce costs by eliminating inefficiencies in litigation. It is a coordinated approach to overseeing and directing all phases of a lawsuit or legal dispute, from its inception to resolution, encompassing tasks like developing legal strategies, managing budgets, coordinating legal teams, and managing documents and evidence. It is an art that integrates strategy, coordination, and foresight. Figure 8.2 shows a representation of litigation management [5].

Figure 8.2 Representation of litigation management [5].

Litigation management requires a methodical approach which can be understood by examining the distinct stages or "pillars" that collectively define the process. Each pillar represents a crucial phase or aspect of litigation, guiding organizations from start to finish. The ten pillars of litigation management are the following [6,7]:

1. *Case Assessment:* At the heart of any litigation lies a case assessment. This involves evaluating the merits of a case, estimating potential damages, and understanding the probability

of success. The assessment phase starts with a listening ear. We learn about our client's business, industry, concerns, and legal needs, and identify what a "win" looks like to our client. Figure 8.3 illustrates case assessment [8].

Figure 8.3 Case assessment [8].

2. *Strategy Development:* This step will consider both legal and business implications. It begins after we have thoroughly analyzed all options for a client. We then present options and partner with the client to develop a strategic defense plan. While the legal strategy aims to win the case or reach a favorable settlement, the business aspect considers the wider implications, like reputation and financial impact.

3. *Budgeting and Cost Management:* Managing costs involves setting a budget, monitoring expenses, and adjusting when necessary. When creating that budget, ensure that effective technology solutions, automation, and continuous process improvement are built into the overall plan. Make sure there are budgets in place that correspond to the project plan. The budget should be based on the list of tasks to be done and who will do them.

4. *Document and Evidence Management:* eDiscovery plays a pivotal role here, focusing on the identification, collection, processing, review, and production of electronic evidence. As litigation often involves the extensive review of documents and data, eDiscovery platforms have emerged as specialized

tools aimed at simplifying this aspect of the process. Proper documentation, cataloging, and storage ensure that relevant electronic and non-electronic evidence can be retrieved and used effectively throughout the litigation process.

5. *Communication and Coordination:* Keeping all stakeholders informed is key. This means coordinating between in-house legal teams, outside counsel, and other relevant departments within an organization. You have to start with and maintain an open line of communication between the risk manager or claims litigation manager and the trial attorney. With good communication, you can eliminate most surprises, whether you deal with one case a year or hundreds.

6. *Risk Management:* This step is to constantly assess the risks involved in litigation, weigh them against potential rewards, and adjust the strategy accordingly. The better organized you are, the easier litigation is to manage.

7. *Oversight of Trial and Post-Trial Processes:* If a case does proceed to trial, managing the presentation of evidence, exhibit list exchanges, witness testimonies, and legal arguments is crucial.

8. *Wise Attorney Selection:* Many resources will provide useful leads for checking the background, credentials, and specialties of attorneys and law firms. Network with industry colleagues. Chat with counterparts at other comparable businesses. Use forums such as claim association or meetings and conferences to learn about high-caliber lawyers and firms. Approach the attorney selection process systematically.

9. *Cost Control:* To help manage costs, have written guidelines for outside defense attorneys. Written guidelines also avoid misunderstandings. They should cover items such as the hourly rates you will pay for partner and associate work, the format and frequency of billings, any budgeting and expense-forecasting requirements, what you will and will not pay for, your policy on legal research and retention of expert witnesses, and what they must get approved by you first.

10. *Service Management:* Written expectations—clearly communicated to outside counsel—are the linchpin of service management. Litigation guidelines should cover not just billing issues, but also service standards. They should provide the framework for your client's "Bill of Rights." Be the architect of your own sound foundation by focusing on these pillars of effective litigation management.

8.4 LITIGATION MANAGEMENT SOFTWARE

Attorneys have mountains of paperwork that includes forms, evidence, emails, recordings, pictures. With multiple court hearings dates of different cases, no lawyer can remember every event in a case. Most legal professionals lack efficiency and productivity due to not having streamlined workflow management. That is where the litigation management tool steps in.

Litigation management solution is software designed to tackle all litigation cases from different jurisdictions. It is a powerful tool that stores all documents, court dates, case titles, opposite party details, and many more in a single software. It is designed to effectively tackle all litigation procedures and cases from different jurisdictions. Figure 8.4 shows litigation management solution [9].

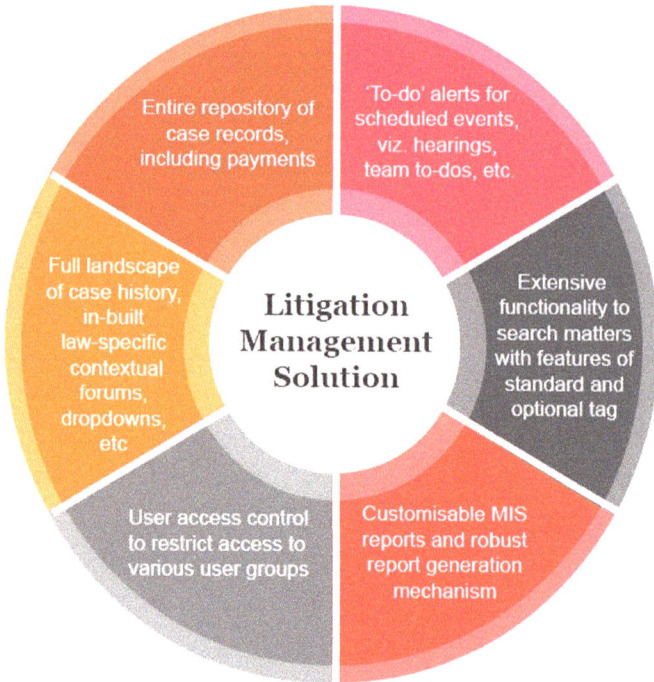

Figure 8.4 Litigation management solution [9].

Litigation management software (LMS) is a cloud-based solution that serves as a central repository for a company's claims that are in litigation. Case-related notices, strategy, dates, details, activities, contact information and files live within this software. Every data related to the litigation process, from hearing dates to contact details, court days, detail is packed in a single feature of litigation management software that ensures enhanced collaboration and insightful decision-making. LMS allows lawyers to keep all of these important details in one centralized place [10]. Claims organizations and risk managers are beginning to migrate toward litigation management software. Perhaps the most significant benefit of litigation management software is that it facilitates the use of structured data that helps claims organizations make better decisions that affect case outcomes and close cases faster [11]. Various software programs such as Freshsales, ServeManager, Rimus, TheLawAssis, etc. are some of the LMS's available for purchase,

8.5 BENEFITS

Accountability in the court of law is the defining aspect of a civilized society. Proper documentation, or lack thereof, can make or break a case. Litigations cause hurdles to enterprises if left unmanaged. Proper management ensures effectively when dealing with matters as complex as litigations. A litigation management system is a profitable investment for the long-term. Following are other benefits of implementing a litigation management solution [12,13]:

• *Central Repository:* A litigation or dispute comprises of a multiplicity of varying petitions, appeals, drafts, notices, etc. Your litigation management system would need to have a central library or a central repository within which to store cases and all ancillary data relating to those cases. The consolidation of various functionalities into a single platform eliminates the need for multiple, specialized tools. This not only streamlines workflows but also reduces the financial burden of licensing multiple pieces of software. With everything in one place, gaps in information are less likely, thereby enhancing strategic planning and decision-making.

• *Saving in the Cloud:* Saving the copies of your documents in a local drive could spell doom if ever there arises a technical error for the computer in which all these files exist and work in. It behooves us to adopt cloud-based approaches to storing our data. The security benefits of online legal software have closed the gaps by way of multiple online methods of data security and back up resources, making cloud-based software solutions an easy alternative to pick with confidence

• *Delegation:* There are responsibilities and duties that arise from the circumstances of each case, and it is not humanly possible to stay on top of every activity in every case. Delegation is the way to route obligations arising from these responsibilities and duties. Task based assignment of your case obligations ensures a fitting response is doled out to address each point of friction.

• *Meeting Deadlines:* It is a tedious task for a law firm to manage all the deadlines, which is an essential part of any case. The thought of having to keep up with the sheer number of updates regarding multiple cases itself is something that strikes fear. With a litigation management tool that provides intelligent updates relating to court procedures and hearings you can be at ease, knowing that no updates regarding your cases will go unnoticed. A litigation management system will merge with the calendaring system in the Microsoft office. It will help you in managing the deadlines more promptly and accurately.

• *Referrals:* All the lawyers or law firms agree that improving client service is a priority for their organizations. To attract and retain customers, you need to satisfy your clients. A satisfied client will always return to the same firm and also refer their family and friends. If an enterprise is looking for ways to improve its customer base, the first investment must be made on a case management system or litigation management system. Your law firm will stay ahead in the competition by using a litigation management system.

• *Collaboration:* Litigation management software can also facilitate much better collaboration and communication, with both claims professionals and attorneys working in one unified platform. A dedicated platform provides a centralized repository for all case-related data and documents, facilitating real-time collaboration among team members and even between in-house and external counsel. This lets you collaborate with paralegals and any other parties involved by setting open folder permissions for your team. Since all the client information is put in one place, it becomes easier to look out for the required contact information.

• *Archiving:* Lawyers need to sift through tremendous amounts of documentation to avoid making mistakes. The law requires that all legal documents be kept in an archive for both active and closed cases. Legal documents need to be archived very carefully in compliance with the law.

8.6 CHALLENGES

In today's litigious business and legal environment, clients face many challenges in litigation management. Insurers, claim professionals, and risk managers have vast legal needs. Managing litigation has always been a significant component of corporate legal practice, but its complexity has intensified over the years. Law firms and corporations that do have dedicated technology specialists tend to be larger. Other challenges include the following [5,8,14]:

• *Security:* Another point of concern is the issue of data security. Homegrown systems may lack the sophisticated encryption and security protocols that specialized litigation management systems offer, making them a risky option for storing sensitive data. Any litigation document management software needs to be able to enforce privacy and integrity of a client's legal documentation.

• *Lack of Scalability:* These systems may also lack scalability and real-time collaboration in matters where you need to share documents and work product with external co-counsel users in real-time. The ideal litigation management platform should not only meet your organization's current needs but also adapt and scale as those needs evolve.

• *Lack of Accountability:* There is a lack of an accountability system when it comes to the judiciary, especially in developing countries like India. It is not only exempted from the preview of the Right to Information Act, but also the permission of chief justice needs to be taken before a case can be instituted against a sitting judge. This hinders the administration of justice in a big way.

• *Technological Issues:* Due to the outbreak of Covid-19 physical courts operational, cases are being heard through video conferencing. Some lawyers are trying to take undue advantage of lockdown. The legal profession is gradually being attempted to be highjacked by a few blessed lawyers and selected law-firms who have high-level connections.

• *Establish Trust and Loyalty:* By using the same firms repeatedly, the attorneys get to know the organization better and can be more effective at staffing and handling cases. The client has to trust the managing attorney to know who is best suited for a specific task. For example, a more experienced attorney may be able to write a brief on a complex subject in far less time than an associate, even at a higher billing rate.

• *Expect Regular Updates:* Although the value and complexity of the case will vary, try to have a uniform approach about status updates. Build monthly updates into the plan with the expectation that updates will occur whenever something happens in the case, such as a filed motion or a judge ruling on the motion. Review and update the budget and the schedule when the case takes an unexpected turn. You also can use the reports available in your litigation management system to review the status of a case at any time.

• *Over-Lawyering:* Getting your lawyers to stay within your budget is only part of the solution. In many cases, the real culprit in runaway litigation costs is over-lawyering, overstaffing a case with too many lawyers and allowing high-priced senior lawyers doing what junior lawyers or paralegals could do far more cheaply.

• *High Fees:* High fees are being charged by lawyers. It has almost become a trend among advocates to charge unnecessarily high fees.

8.7 CONCLUSION

With the growing world and its technology, it is important for law firms to adopt new ways to deal with the competition. The management of clients and their cases is vital to be considered as the core. Litigation is the process of taking a dispute to a law court to resolve it. It is the process of resolving disputes through the legal system, which can take anywhere from a few months to several years, depending on the case's complexity and other factors. Litigation management refers to the coordinated approach to overseeing and directing all phases of a lawsuit or legal dispute, from the beginning through to its resolution. It often boils down to lawyer management. Lawyers can and should be managed, just like any other outside service vendor: a broker, a third-party administrator, or a safety consultant. It is possible to manage litigation to save time, money, and frustration. It is important to note that today's best practices are tomorrow's legacy systems. More information on litigation management is available from the books in [15-17] and a related magazine: *Litigation Management Magazine.*

REFERENCE

[1] "What is litigation management?" October 2023,

https://www.tcdi.com/what-is-litigation-management/

[2] M. N. O. Sadiku, P. A. Adekunte, and J. O. Sadiku, "Litigation management," *International Journal of Trend in Scientific Research and Development*, vol. 9, no. 2, March-April 2025, pp. 805-811.

[3] A. Sullivan, "What does litigation mean?" April 2021,

https://bluesteinattorneys.com/what-does-litigation-mean/

[4] "What is litigation and how long should it take?" Unknown Source.

[5] "Comparing technology & software for litigation management," January 2024,

https://www.tcdi.com/comparing-technology-software-for-litigation-management/

[6] "Litigation manager resume: Job description, sample & guide,"

https://resumaker.ai/resume-examples/litigation-manager/

[7] M. Boutot, "The three pillars of litigation management," February 2008,

https://www.irmi.com/articles/expert-commentary/the-three-pillars-of-litigation-management

[8] R. Donlon, "8 Best practices for claims litigation management," April 2015,

https://www.propertycasualty360.com/2015/04/30/8-best-practices-for-claims-litigation-management/?slretu rn=20250326195307

[9] "Litigation management solution,"

https://www.pwc.in/tax-knowledge-hub/navigate-tax/litigation-management-solution.html

[10] https://www.mattersuite.com/blog/build-a-perfect-workflow-with-litigation-management-software/

[11] "Litigation management software 101," September 2021,

https://caseglide.com/blog/litigation-management-software-101/

[12] "Litigation document management software," May 2020,

https://www.folderit.com/blog/litigation-document-management-software/

[13] "5 Benefits of implementing a litigation management solution," July 2021,

https://lexplosion.in/5-benefits-of-implementing-a-litigation-management-solution/

[14] "Is litigation management software hitting a tipping point?"

https://vidmaconsulting.com/is-litigation-management-software-hitting-a-tipping-point/

[15] J. M. Custis, *Litigation Management Handbook*, 2023-2024 ed. Clark Boardman Callaghan, 2023.

[16] C. E. Harris II, *Emerging Trends in Litigation Management.* *Full Court Press*, 2020.

[17] Federal Judicial Center. Information Services Office, *Civil Litigation Management Manual*. Administrative Office of the United States Courts, 2010.

CHAPTER 9
IDENTITY MANAGEMENT

"No man is above the law, and no man is below it; nor do we ask any man's permission when we require him to obey it."

—Theodore Roosevelt

9.1 INTRODUCTION

With digital transformation gaining even more momentum, their protection is an absolute must. In the era of digital transformation, digital identity management emerges as a key enabler for organizations seeking to enhance cybersecurity, strengthen customer trust, and comply with regulatory requirements.

Today, data is the most valuable commodity in the world. This is reflected by the ever-increasing number of cyberattacks. Evolving cyber threats have increased the risk of online identities becoming compromised. As a result, traditional user authentication methods (using username and password, biometrics, etc.) have proven to be lacking. Identity management emerged as a solution to the limitations of traditional identity verification methods. It refers to the processes and technologies used to manage and secure information about the identity of individuals or entities within a digital system. It is the organizational process for ensuring individuals have the appropriate access to technology resources.

Organizations of all sizes rely on a variety of tools and technologies to function and compete in today's digital world. Identity management encompasses the processes involved in securing and overseeing unique digital representations of people and devices. For them to protect their systems, data, and resources, identity management best practices are essential. By adhering to these best practices, organizations can make sure that their identity management systems are efficient at safeguarding their resources, data, and systems while also preserving the confidence of their clients and other stakeholders.

Identity management refers to how an organization identifies and authenticates individuals for access to its networks or applications. The process ensures that individuals and groups have the right access, rights, and restrictions with established identities for the organizational resources while keeping their assets and data secure. Identity management is important because it aids in preventing security events like data leaks and illegal access. From logging into email and collaboration platforms to accessing corporate resources, identity management plays a pivotal role in daily interactions online [1].

In this chapter, we will explore the role of identity management solutions in securing users and devices. The chapter begins with explaining the concepts of digital identity and identity management. It discusses identity and access management. It highlights the benefits and challenges of identity management. The last section concludes with comments.

9.2 WHAT IS A DIGITAL IDENTITY?

An identity is the collection of unique characteristics that define a person, organization, resource or a service in conjunction with any optional additional information. A digital identity is the information and data that identifies an individual in the digital world. It consists of a set of attributes and credentials, such as name, date of birth, e-mail address, and biometrics, as well as certificates, passwords, or other cryptographic keys. Digital identities are typically stored in a central database or directory, which acts as a source of truth. We all have some sort of digital presence, social media, e-mail, etc. which can all be described as our individual digital identities. Within the corporate world, it is the organizational identity which matters and therefore forms the core of the identities of users within the infrastructure.

Digital identities have become a core element of a company's DNA. An employee ID allows the workforce of a company to access the internal network and enables organizations to manage permissions. A consumer ID provides online shoppers with increased security while allowing providers to gather insights into user preferences and demographics. An e-banking ID (a special form of consumer ID) can be used to access online banking services, view account information, and make transactions. A citizen ID offers secure 24/7 access to government services online, encouraging digital use and reducing the need for office [2]. Figure 9.1 shows these forms of ID [2].

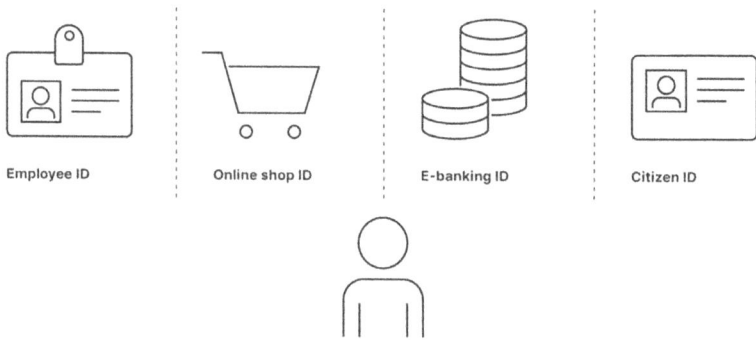

Employee ID   Online shop ID   E-banking ID   Citizen ID

Figure 9.1 Some forms of ID [2].

9.3 WHAT IS IDENTITY MANAGEMENT?

Identity management (IDM) is an identity security framework that works to authenticate and authorize user access to resources such as applications, data, systems, and cloud platforms. It is a framework for policies and technologies that ensure the secure management of digital identities, focusing on identifying, authenticating, and authorizing users and applications to access internal resources. It is a method of verifying the identities of network entities and the level of access for enterprise network resources. Its main goal is to ensure only authenticated users are granted access to the specific applications, systems or IT environments for which they are authorized. At the core of an identity management system are policies defining which devices and users are allowed on the network and what a user can accomplish, depending on device type, location, and other factors.

Identity management systems must enable companies to automatically manage multiple users in different situations and computing environments in real time. They include software, hardware, and procedures used to identify and authorize a person or persons that need access to applications, systems, networks, or physical locations. They encompass the tools, protocols, and practices used to establish, validate, and maintain digital identities. This is done by first ensuring that the right person or persons are identified, and then verifying that those persons are authorized to access the item or resource in question. Identity management aids in ensuring compliance with laws and industry standards pertaining to data protection and privacy. Figure 9.2 shows a representation of identity management [2].

Figure 9.2 A representation of identity management [2].

There are a number of identity management systems available today that perform a few key functions. They are displayed in Figure 9.3 [3] and briefly explained as follows [3]:

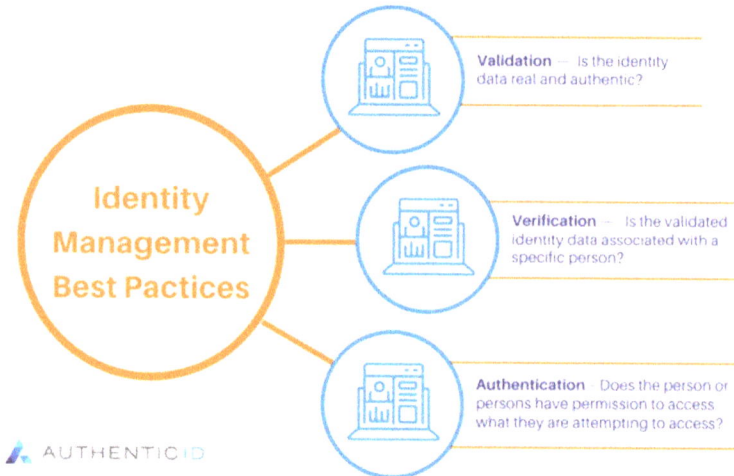

Figure 9.3 Key functions of identity management systems [3].

- Validation – Is the identity data real and authentic?

- Verification – This verifies the identity of users through credentials or other means. Is the validated identity data associated with a specific person?

- Authentication – This involves verifying the identity of users or entities attempting to access a system. Does the person or persons have permission to access what they are attempting to access?

A driver's license is an example of identity data. Other examples may include biometric data (fingerprints, facial recognition, selfies, etc.), documents (passports or government-issued ID), challenge questions, or even behavioral signals. Organizations may use a variety of these methods within their identity management process. Figure 9.4 shows various means of identifying a person [4].

Figure 9.4 Various means of identifying a person [4].

9.4 IDENTITY AND ACCESS MANAGEMENT

In addition to managing employees, use of identity management along with access management enables businesses to manage customer, partner, supplier, and device access to their systems while ensuring security. The terms "identity management" and "access management" are often used interchangeably or in combination. But a distinction does exist between the two concepts. Identity management focuses on managing the attributes related to the user, group of users, devices, or other network entities that require access to resources. In contrast, access management focuses on evaluating user or device attributes based on an organization's existing policies and governance. Identity access management (IAM) is an umbrella term that encompasses all of the processes involved in identifying people inside a system and restricts access to such information to only authorized users [5]. IAM systems fall under the overarching umbrellas of IT security and data management. Identity and access management (IAM) ensures that the right people (identity) can access the right resources at the right times, for the right reasons (access management). The purpose of IAM is to stop hackers while allowing authorized users to easily do everything they need to do. Organizations of all sizes need IAM solutions to make sure that only authorized people have access to the systems. Figure 9.5 represents identity and access management [4], while Figure 9.6 presents some IAM tools [6]. A typical IAM system has a database or a directory of users.

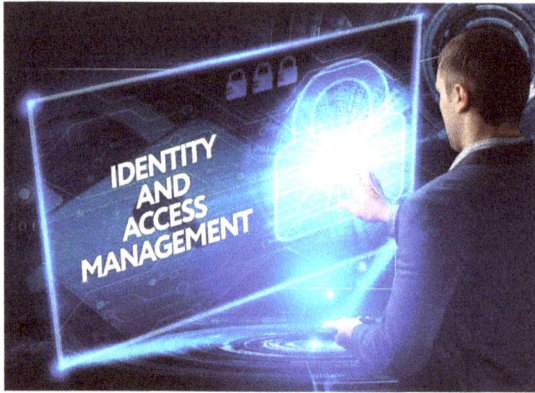

Figure 9.5 Representation of identity and access management [4].

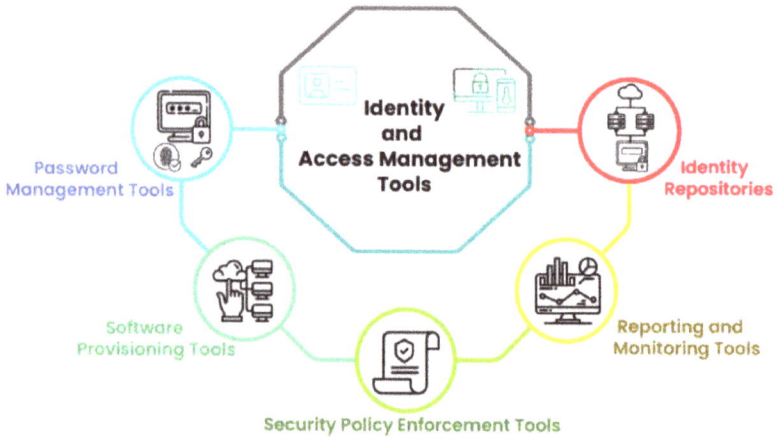

Figure 9.6 Some IAM tools [6].

Thanks to IAM, users can use their digital identity to gain access to different systems. Any corporation that wants to safeguard its resources, data, and systems must have a strong IAM strategy. Unauthorized access, data breaches, and other security problems can all be avoided with the help of an efficient IAM approach. Implementing appropriate security measures to guard against data breaches and other security threats is another critical component of an IAM strategy.

There are two types of IAM, centralized and decentralized identity management models [7]:

- *Centralized identity and access management* (IAM) is a framework for storing and managing users' identity data in a single location. It consolidates the storage and exchange of users' login credentials and privileges. It provides a secure process for identifying, authenticating, and authorizing users who have permission to access a company's digital assets. With centralized IAM, users can access all the resources and applications they need to do their jobs by entering only one set of login credentials. Critics of a centralized approach often cite the single identity store as the most troubling issue. Relying on a single set of credentials creates a single point of failure.

- *Distributed identity management* (also known as decentralized authentication), allows users access applications individually using a different set of credentials for each. This model distributes users' identities across the network, as each application must store and handle its own user data. Decentralized identity management gives users more control but offers companies less visibility. It eliminates single point of failure by distributing data and increasing trust. Decentralized IAM relies on nascent Web3 technologies—specifically blockchain and user-owned, decentralized identifiers (DID). DIDs allow users to control their data and offer a convenient way to authenticate with a wide range of applications.

Since there is no need for consensus across a large network, decentralized solutions are typically less expensive.

9.5 APPLICATIONS OF IDENTITY MANAGEMENT

Identity management (IDM) in essence refers to the management or administration of individual identities within a system, such as a company or network. It encompasses a variety of components and practices, including authentication, authorization, and identity governance. Innovations in the user identity management space have been a trend in the past couple of years. Specific applications of identity management include the following [8]:

• *Biometric Authentication:* Biometric authentication ensures a seamless and convenient user experience while minimizing the risk of unauthorized access. New techniques in biometric authentication include advanced methods such as vein pattern recognition, gait analysis, and behavioral biometrics (such as typing patterns or mouse movements) to enhance security and usability. Digital identity management will also witness advancements in biometric authentication, leveraging unique biological traits for secure verification. Technologies like facial recognition, iris scanning, and fingerprint authentication are already prevalent.

• *Blockchain Technology:* Blockchain provides a decentralized and tamper-proof ledger, ensuring that each user's identity information is stored in a block that's cryptographically linked to the previous one. This decentralized approach makes data breaches much more difficult.

• *Two-Factor Authentication:* Two-factor authentication (2FA) adds an extra layer of security by requiring users to provide two different forms of identification, like a PIN code or QR code sent to the user's registered phone. Multi-factor authentication (MFA) requires users to provide two or more authentication factors to prove their identities. Combined with multifactor authentication and enforceable security policies, enterprises can lower the risk of security breaches.

• *Zero Trust Architecture:* This assumes that no user or device can be trusted by default, regardless of their location. It enforces strict access controls, continuous monitoring, and least privilege principles. Identity is not only the most important element in Zero

Trust; identity is the new perimeter.

• *Encryption:* Digital identity systems employ robust encryption with a public and private key cryptographic authentication system, preventing unauthorized access to networks and data as only the intended user has the private key used to decrypt the message.

• *IDM in the Workplace:* Identity governance and administration (IGA) solutions ensure that all identities in an organization get the right access to the right resources. Organizations with simpler needs choose light IGA solutions with a subset of IGA features to reduce cost and deployment time. Light IGA solutions often focus on identity administration features.

• *Single sign-on (SSO):* SSO allows users to access multiple apps and services with one set of login credentials. The SSO portal authenticates the user and generates a certificate or token that acts as a security key for other resources. SSO systems use open protocols like Security Assertion Markup Language (SAML) to share keys freely between different service providers. Features like SSO and adaptive access allow users to authenticate with minimal friction while protecting vital assets.

• *Cloud Identity Management:* This is the subsequent step of identity and access management (IAM) solutions. However, it is a lot more than merely a straightforward web app single sign-on (SSO) solution. Identity management in cloud computing incorporates all categories of user-base who can operate in diverse scenarios and with specific devices. Identity management in cloud computing is highly critical to an organization. This next generation of IAM solution is a holistic move of the identity provider right to the cloud. Cloud IAM solutions provide a clean and single access control interface. Figure 9.7 shows the representation of cloud IDM [9].

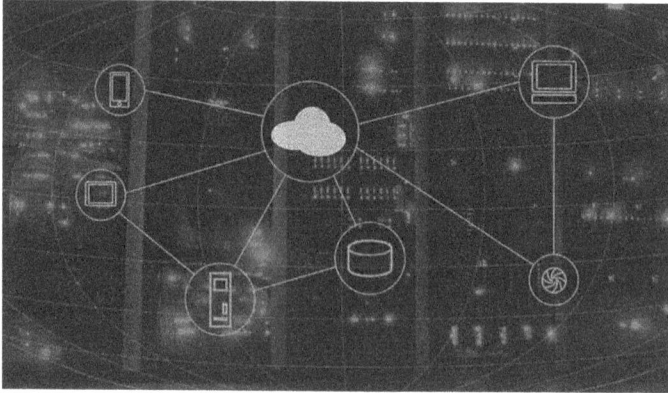

Figure 9.7 Representation of cloud IDM [9].

9.6 BENEFITS

A major benefit of identity management is the ability to efficiently carry out transactions and complete tasks like document signing. Users can effortlessly access various online services without the need to remember different passwords or usernames. Identity management is indispensable for maintaining security, ensuring user trust, and meeting regulatory standards in today's digital landscape. Embracing it can significantly improve the security of your organization and optimize workflow while keeping your mission-critical data secure. Other benefits include the following [2]:

• *Automation:* Many key IAM workflows are hard or outright impossible to do manually. Instead, organizations rely on technology tools to automate IAM processes. Modern IDM and IAM systems frequently have automated features that help ensure controls are in place to manage these risks. These systems also help to manage compliance with an ever-changing ecosystem of regulations that ensure users only have access to authorized data, and that data lives in the right place.

• *Competitive Advantage:* In a fast-paced business environment, being able to quickly adapt and integrate advanced identity management solutions can provide a competitive edge, improving security, operational efficiency, and customer trust.

• *Identity Governance:* This is the process of tracking what users do with access rights. Identity governance provides oversight and monitoring, helping organizations track and manage who has access to specific resources and why. IAM systems monitor users to ensure that they do not abuse their privileges and to catch hackers who may have snuck into the network. Identity governance is important for regulatory compliance.

• *Less Reliance on Physical Documents:* Traditional identity systems rely on physical documents (e.g., driver's licenses, passports) for verification. Digital identity management eliminates the need for physical documents, reducing the risk of theft or loss.

• *Cybersecurity:* A reason that IAM is important is that cybercriminals are evolving their methods daily. Identity management plays a vital role in protecting organizations against breaches. By implementing stringent access controls and continuously monitoring identity activities, organizations can mitigate the risk of cyberattacks and data leaks. This not only protects the organization's assets but also upholds its reputation and trustworthiness. While perfect protection unfortunately is not possible, IAM solutions are an excellent way to prevent and minimize the impact of attacks. While no security system is infallible, using IAM technology significantly reduces your risk of data breaches.

• *Cost Efficiency:* While initial setup may be expensive, managing digital identities in-house can lead to long-term cost savings by reducing reliance on third-party services.

• *Productivity:* Identity management can improve employee productivity. This is especially important when onboarding new employees or changing authorizations for accessing different systems when an employee's function changes. As tempting as it might be to implement a complicated security system to prevent breaches, having multiple barriers to productivity like multiple logins and passwords is a frustrating user experience.

• *Delegation:* Delegation enables local administrators or supervisors to perform system modifications without a global administrator or for one user to allow another to perform actions on their behalf. For example, a user could delegate the right to manage office-related information.

• *Improved Collaboration:* Seamless collaboration between employees, vendors, contractors, and suppliers is essential to keeping up with the pace of modern work. IAM enables this collaboration by making sure that not only is collaboration secure, it is also fast and easy.

9.7 CHALLENGES

Identity management comes with numerous challenges affecting all levels of an organization. Merging modern IAM technology with existing legacy infrastructures is not always easy. People are tired of creating and managing all of their user ID and password combinations. Other challenges include the following [2]:

• *Password Management:* One of the top challenges in implementing identity management is password management. IT professionals should invest in techniques that reduce the impact of password issues in their companies. They must enforce strong password policies and manage password resets. Employees often cannot remember and maintain multiple secure passwords to access the resources they need to get their jobs done. By streamlining communication processes and access control, identity management not only improves IT security, it improves the user experience as well.

• *Resource Shortages:* When it comes to identity management, two types of resources can lead to problems if there is a shortage of them. Firstly, human resources are an issue, as securely managing digital identities requires a broad range of qualified professionals which are hard to find. Secondly, financial resources play a key role. Smaller companies or those with limited IT budgets may struggle to allocate sufficient funds for hiring, training, and retaining IAM professionals or investing in necessary technologies.

• *Complexity:* The complexity of identity management consists of several interrelated factors further emphasizing the need for highly skilled employees. Identity management needs to be integrated across a variety of systems, applications, and platforms, each with its own requirements and protocols. To meet the complex use cases of modern enterprises, IAM platforms must integrate with a wide variety of systems.

• *Security:* Protecting against a wide range of security threats, such as phishing, brute force attacks, and insider threats, requires advanced security measures and continuous vigilance. With new technologies and vulnerabilities, new attack vectors emerge. Quickly implementing updated security measures helps organizations stay ahead of these threats. In-house management ensures that all identity processes align with the latest global data privacy and security regulations.

• *Scalability:* Ensuring that the identity management system can scale to accommodate growth, additional users, and increased data without compromising performance or security adds another layer of complexity. As a company grows, it might struggle to scale their systems efficiently, leading to performance issues and operational bottlenecks. Standard solutions are built to scale according to the needs of the business, allowing for easy adjustments as the company grows or changes.

• *Interoperability:* Achieving interoperability between different identity management solutions and standards involves careful planning and implementation.

• *Regulatory Compliance:* Keeping up with evolving regulations and industry standards can be difficult, increasing the risk of non-compliance and potential legal penalties. Regulations and compliance standards are frequently updated to address new security concerns and protect user data. Companies must adapt quickly to meet these evolving requirements and avoid legal penalties. Ensuring that identity management practices comply with ever increasing regulations involves ongoing monitoring, auditing, and reporting.

• *Access Control:* Users expect easy and quick access. This can conflict with the need for robust security measures, which is also increasingly a hard requirement for most users. Defining and enforcing granular access control policies necessitates detailed planning and constant updates.

• *Flexibility:* With emerging methodologies, business requirements are changing rapidly, adapting to market trends, responding to customer needs, and necessitating an update of the IT strategy. Therefore, identity management systems need to be flexible to accommodate new projects, technologies, or organizational changes.

• *Data Privacy:* One major concern with identity management is data privacy. Keeping data secure and private is not easy. Customers demand that the companies they do business with not only make their personal experiences enjoyable, but that those companies keep their data safe from breaches and protect their privacy. Fragmented global data and privacy regulation is creating compliance challenges. As a result of the growing list of breaches, violations of customer privacy, and increasing consumer dissatisfaction, there has been an explosion of regulations related to data security and privacy.

• *Cost:* Managing digital identities requires significant investment in technology and infrastructure, which can strain the limited resources of smaller companies.

• *Lack of Expertise:* There may be a lack of the specialized knowledge required to effectively manage digital identities, leading to potential misconfigurations, security gaps, and operational inefficiencies.

9.8 CONCLUSION

Identity management (IDM) essentially refers to the management or administration of individual identities within a system, such as a company or network. Today, the importance of an effective IDM strategy cannot be overstated. In the digital age, where digital interactions are everywhere, users must be able to trust that their identities and personal information are protected. Effective digital identity management provides this assurance by verifying that users are who they claim to be through strong authentication methods. For those who want to master or speed up digital transformation, the key is to thoroughly manage and protect digital identities on all levels. IDM can and should be a key component of a business's security and productivity strategies [10]. By falling short on IAM best practices, organizations unknowingly risk their own security, along with that of their customers and shareholders. More information on identity management is available from the books in [11-21].

REFERENCE

[1] M. N. O. Sadiku, P. A. Adekunte, and J. O. Sadiku, "Identity management," *International Journal of Trend in Scientific Research and Development*, vol. 9, no. 2, March-April 2025, pp. 788-796.

[2] "What is digital identity management and how do you master it?"

https://www.adnovum.com/blog/digital-identity-management

[3] "Identity management," Unknown Source.

[4] T. Watson, "What is identity management – Its characteristics & benefits," August 2020,

https://skywell.software/blog/identity-management-characteristics-benefits/

[5] "What is identity management (ID management)?"

https://www.techtarget.com/searchsecurity/definition/identity-management-ID-management

[6] E. Wisniowska, "Top 10 best IAM tools – Identity access management (pros cons)," November 2022,

https://infrasos.com/top-10-best-iam-tools-identity-access-management/

[7] S. Brown, "Centralized and decentralized identity management explained,"

https://www.strongdm.com/blog/centralized-decentralized-identity-management

[8] R. Villano, "Digital identity management: How it's revolutionising user and device authentication," May 2024,

https://www.globalsign.com/en/blog/sg/digital-identity-management-how-its-revolutionizing-user-and-device-authentication

[9] R. Soni, "Identity management in cloud computing," January 2021,

https://www.loginradius.com/blog/identity/identity-management-in-cloud-computing/

[10] J. Barton, "Identity management – What you need to know," June 2015,

https://www.univention.com/blog-en/2015/06/identity-management-what-you-need-to-know/

[11] M. Bryght, *Identity and Access Management: from Zero to Hero: Learn all you need about Identity and Access Management (IAM) (Identity in Cybersecurity)*. Independently Published, 2024.

[12] M. Chapple, *Access Control and Identity Management (Information Systems Security & Assurance)*. Jones & Bartlett Learning, 3rd edition, 2020.

[13] A. Zulejhic, *Identity and Access Management: Fundamentals*. Independently Published, 2022.

[14] E. Sergeev, *Identity Management Crisis: Solving IAM's Biggest Challenges*. Independently Published, 2025.

[15] M. J. Haber and D. Rolls, *Identity Attack Vectors: Implementing an Effective Identity and Access Management Solution*. Apress, 2019.

[16] Y. Wilson and A. Hingnikar, *Solving Identity Management in Modern Applications: Demystifying OAuth 2, OpenID Connect, and SAML 2*. Apress, 2nd edition, 2022.

[17] J. Nickel, *Mastering Identity and Access Management with Microsoft Azure*. Packt Publishing, 2nd edition, 2019.

[18] M. Laurent and S. Bouzefrane, *Digital Identity Management*. ISTE Press - Elsevier, 2015. ·

[19] E. Bertino and K. Takahashi, *Identity Management: Concepts, Technologies, and Systems*. Artech House, 2010.

[20] K. Spaulding et al., *Identity Management: A Primer*. MC Press Online, LLC. 2009.

[21] D. G. W. Birch (ed.), *Digital Identity Management: Perspectives on the Technological, Business and Social Implications*. Gower, 2007.-

CHAPTER 10
CYBERSECURITY IN LAW PRACTICE

"The purpose of the law is to prevent the strong from always having their way."

—Ovid

10.1 INTRODUCTION

In an era dominated by digital advancements, many legal practices have embraced technology to streamline operations, enhance efficiency, and facilitate better communication. However, with the increasing reliance on digital platforms comes the heightened risk of cyber threats. In the era of digital transformation, the legal profession is not immune to the challenges and opportunities that come with it. Cybersecurity remains a top concern in the legal profession. Lawyers are entrusted with sensitive information, making them prime targets for cyber threats. They must take steps to protect their own security and privacy, as well as that of their clients. Maintaining a strong cybersecurity posture is crucial for safeguarding the legal professional reputation.

Hackers often target law firms due to the wealth of valuable information they possess, ranging from personal client details to sensitive case strategies. A successful cyber-attack can not only compromise the privacy of clients but also erode the trust and credibility of the legal profession as a whole [1].

Cybersecurity is the protection of systems and information connected to the Internet. It refers to the measures taken to protect systems, networks, and data from digital attacks. Cybersecurity breaches for law firms are like others in the industry. Hackers are increasingly targeting law firms because they can become a one-stop shop for a variety of sensitive documents and a gold mine of information. With cyber-attacks ranking as the fifth highest risk, the need for cybersecurity measures in law firms has become imperative. Cybersecurity and data protection play a significant role in the legal profession. They have become a critical aspect of the legal profession since lawyers are bound by various laws and regulations that mandate the protection of their client data. Cybersecurity in the legal sector is no longer a dispensable luxury but an indispensable necessity [2].

This chapter aims to explore the complex landscape of cybersecurity in the legal industry. It begins with providing an overview of cybersecurity. It discusses cybersecurity in the legal industry and how to combat it. It describes cybersecurity attorney. It highlights the benefits and challenges of cybersecurity in the legal industry. The last section concludes with comments.

10.2 OVERVIEW OF CYBERSECURITY

Cybersecurity refers to a set of technologies and practices designed to protect networks and information from damage or unauthorized access. It is vital because governments, companies, and military organizations collect, process, and store a lot of data. As shown in Figure 10.1, cybersecurity involves multiple issues related to people, process, and technology [3]. Figure 10.2 shows different components of cybersecurity [4].

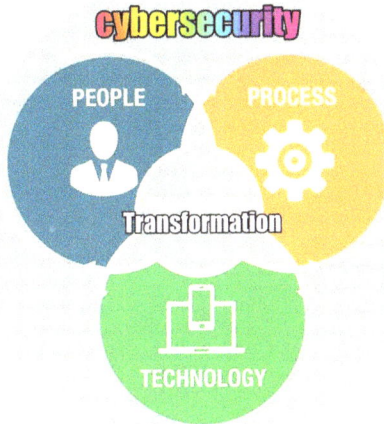

Figure 10.1 Cybersecurity involves multiple issues related to people, process, and technology [3].

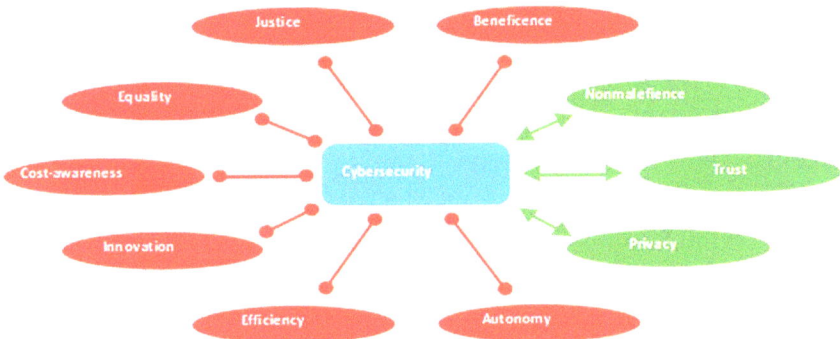

Figure 10.2 Different components of cybersecurity [4].(Green: supportive; red: in tension).

A typical cyber attack is an attempt by adversaries or cybercriminals to gain access to and modify their target's computer system or network. Cybercriminals or ethical hackers are modern-day digital warriors, possessing extraordinary skills and knowledge to breach even the most impregnable systems. A typical cybercriminal is shown on Figure 10.3 [5].

Figure 10.3 A typical cybercriminal [5].

Cyber attacks are becoming more frequent, sophisticated, dangerous, and destructive. They are threatening the operation of businesses, banks, companies, and government networks. They vary from illegal crime of individual citizen (hacking) to actions of groups (terrorists) [6].

Cybersecurity is a dynamic, interdisciplinary field involving information systems, computer science, and criminology. The security objectives have been availability, authentication, confidentiality, nonrepudiation, and integrity. A security incident is an act that threatens the confidentiality, integrity, or availability of information assets and systems [7]. These are known as the pillars of information assurance.

- *Availability:* This refers to availability of information and ensuring that authorized parties can access the information when needed. Attacks targeting availability of service generally leads to denial of service.

- *Authenticity:* This ensures that the identity of an individual user or system is the identity claimed. This usually involves using username and password to validate the identity of the user. It may also take the form of what you have such as a driver's license, an RSA token, or a smart card.

- *Integrity:* Data integrity means information is authentic and complete. This assures that data, devices, and processes are free from tampering. Data should be free from injection, deletion, or corruption. When integrity is targeted, nonrepudiation is also affected.

- *Confidentiality:* Confidentiality ensures that measures are taken to prevent sensitive information from reaching the wrong persons. Data secrecy is important especially for privacy-sensitive data such as user personal information and meter readings.

- *Nonrepudiation:* This is an assurance of the responsibility to an action. The source should not be able to deny having sent a message, while the destination should not deny having received it. This security objective is essential for accountability and liability.

Good practices for cybersecurity in construction companies should include all of these elements.

Everybody is at risk for a cyber attack. Cyber attacks vary from illegal crime of individual citizen (hacking) to actions of groups (terrorists). The following are typical examples of cyber attacks or threats [8]:

- *Malware:* This is a malicious software or code that includes traditional computer viruses, computer worms, and Trojan horse programs. Malware can infiltrate your network through the Internet, downloads, attachments, email, social media, and other platforms. Spyware is a type of malware that collects information without the victim's knowledge.

- *Phishing:* Criminals trick victims into handing over their personal information such as online passwords, social security number, and credit card numbers.

- *Denial-of-Service Attacks:* These are designed to make a network resource unavailable to its intended users. These can prevent the user from accessing email, websites, online accounts or other services.

- *Social Engineering Attacks:* A cyber criminal attempts to trick users to disclose sensitive information. A social engineer aims to convince a user through impersonation to disclose secrets such as passwords, card numbers, or social security number.

- *Man-In-the-Middle Attack:* This is a cyber attack where a malicious attacker secretly inserts him/herself into a conversation between two parties who believe they are directly communicating with each other. A common example of man-in-the-middle attacks is eavesdropping. The goal of such an attack is to steal personal information.

These and other cyber attacks or threats are shown in Figure 10.4 [9]. Sources of cyber threats are displayed in Figure 10.5 [10].

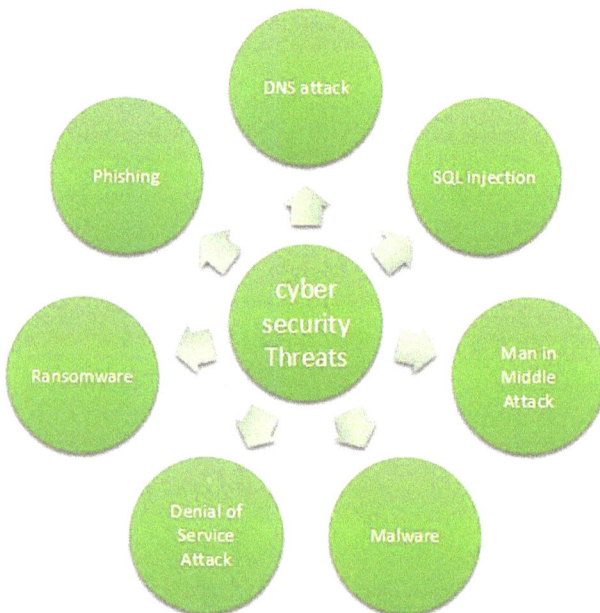

Figure 10.4 Common types of cybersecurity threats [9].

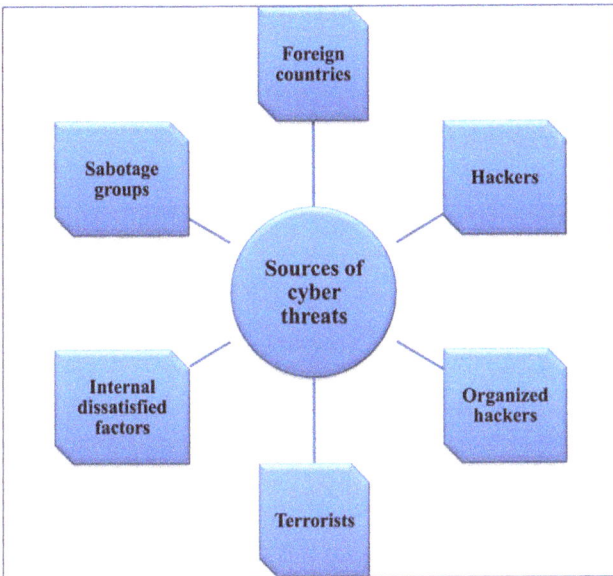

Figure 10.5 Sources of cyber threats [10].

The social and financial importance of cybersecurity is increasingly being recognized by businesses, organizations, and governments. Cybersecurity involves reducing the risk of cyber attacks. Cyber risks should be managed proactively by the management. Cybersecurity technologies such as firewalls are widely available [11]. Cybersecurity is the joint responsibility of all relevant stakeholders including government, business, infrastructure owners, and users. Cybersecurity experts have shown that passwords are highly vulnerable to cyber threats, compromising personal data, credit card records, and even social security numbers. Governments and international organizations play a key role in cybersecurity issues. Securing the cyberspace is of high priority to the US Department of Homeland Security (DHS). Vendors that offer mobile security solutions include Zimperium, MobileIron Skycure, Lookout, and Wandera.

10.3 CYBERSECURITY IN THE LEGAL INDUSTRY

Law firms regularly handle substantial funds and sensitive information. This makes them attractive targets for cyber criminals who engage in social engineering, 'man-in-the-middle' cybercrimes or seek ransoms to prevent the release of confidential information. Legal firms face various cyber threats, including data breaches, ransomware attacks, phishing attempts, insider threats and compromises of vendor data, breach and defacement of websites, social engineering attacks, misconfigured cloud services, and data interception. These breaches bring the risk of unauthorized access, exposure, or theft of sensitive client information. They disrupt regular work, causing financial and reputational harm. A breach can result in the loss of client trust, financial penalties, and even legal repercussions for failing to protect client data [12]. Figure 10.6 shows the top five cyber threats to law firms [13].

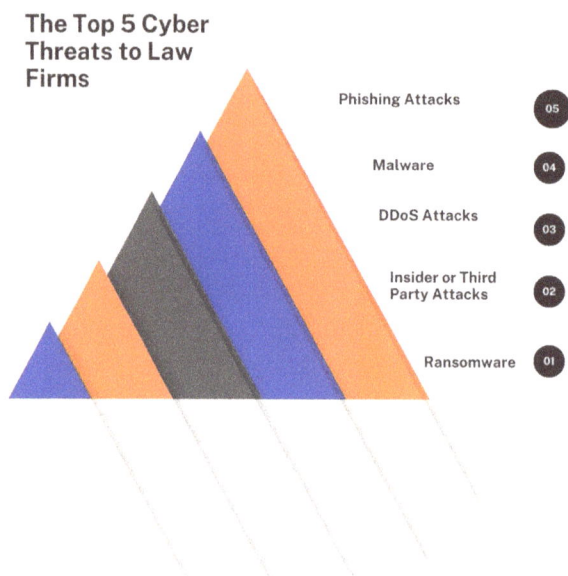

The Top 5 Cyber Threats to Law Firms

Phishing Attacks 05

Malware 04

DDoS Attacks 03

Insider or Third Party Attacks 02

Ransomware 01

Figure 10.6 Top five cyber threats to law firms [13].

Data breaches are not always the result of external attacks; they can also occur due to insider threats, where employees intentionally or unintentionally compromise the security of the firm's data. Cybercriminals might exploit vulnerabilities in a firm's network, gain access through phishing attacks, or even leverage weak passwords to infiltrate systems. Preventing data breaches requires a proactive approach to cybersecurity. In view of this, the technological competency of lawyers has assumed great importance. It is not just a practical necessity but also an ethical duty. Cybersecurity aims to safeguard against unauthorized access, use, disclosure, disruption, modification, or destruction of information. Effective cybersecurity measures are essential for building trust with clients [14].

Legal cybersecurity refers to the strategies, practices, and technologies put in place to protect the data and information systems of legal entities against cyberattacks. It includes securing confidential client files, preventing data breaches, and ensuring compliance with industry rules. Cybersecurity for law firms is necessary to protect the company's information. Figure 10.7 shows a symbol for legal cybersecurity [15]. A greater part of cybersecurity for law firms stores their data in the cloud; however, this demands very tight security measures. Figure 10.8 shows best cybersecurity practices for the law firms [13].

Figure 10.7 A symbol for legal cybersecurity [15].

Best Cybersecurity For Law Firms – Security Defenses

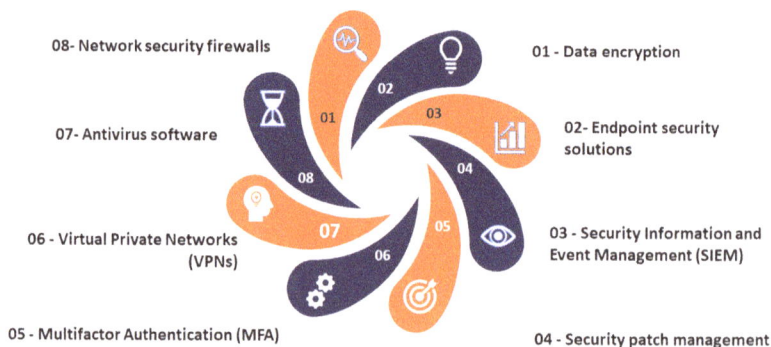

08- Network security firewalls

07- Antivirus software

06 - Virtual Private Networks (VPNs)

05 - Multifactor Authentication (MFA)

01 - Data encryption

02- Endpoint security solutions

03 - Security Information and Event Management (SIEM)

04 - Security patch management

Figure 10.8 Best cybersecurity practices for the law firms [13].

Data protection ensures that personal data are secure, while cybersecurity is broad and enjoins all forms of information, be it sensitive commercial data or private data. Cybersecurity also incorporates data storage, transmission, and retention with security measures as the data is in a state of motion either on a server or hard disk.

Best practices for cybersecurity in the legal sector [16]:

- *Regular Training:* Conduct cybersecurity training for all staff members to raise awareness about potential threats, phishing scams, and best practices

- *Update software and Systems:* Keep all software, including operating systems and legal software applications, up-to-date with the latest security patches. Regularly update and patch systems to address vulnerabilities and reduce the risk of exploitation by cybercriminals.

- *Risk Management:* IT infrastructure and networks should be regularly audited to identify and mitigate specific risks and weaknesses in the cybersecurity posture, and the impact of those threats on business operations.

- *Data Encryption:* Ensure that all sensitive data, including client information, legal documents, and communications, are encrypted.

- *Access Controls & Authentication:* Implement strong access controls and authentication mechanisms to restrict access to sensitive legal information.

- *Backup and Disaster Recovery:* Implement a robust backup and disaster recovery plan to ensure the availability and integrity of legal data in case of a cyberattack or data loss. Regularly test backups to confirm their reliability and establish procedures for quick recovery in the event of a security incident.

- *Incident Response Plan:* Develop and regularly update an incident response plan that outlines the steps to be taken in case of a cybersecurity incident. This includes identifying and containing the breach, notifying affected parties, and implementing measures to prevent future incidents.

10.4 COMBATING CYBERSECURITY IN THE LEGAL INDUSTRY

Parallel to the rise of cybersecurity, the concept of data protection began to take shape. Data protection refers to the practices, safeguards, and binding rules put in place to protect personal data. In the legal context, data protection focuses on the secure collection, storage, and processing of personal data while respecting individuals' rights. It involves implementing policies and procedures to protect personal data from unauthorized access, use, or sharing without proper consent. Data protection holds significant importance for lawyers because legal professionals have legal obligations to protect client data. By implementing robust data protection measures, we can assure clients that their personal data is treated with the utmost care and confidentiality. Any data breach or non-compliance with data protection laws can have severe repercussions, including reputational damage [17].

To combat ever-intensifying cybersecurity threats, there are various types of security defenses that law firms can employ to protect their data and systems. These include the following [18,19]:

1. *Routine Risk Assessments:* A law firm's IT department should conduct ongoing security risk assessments, vulnerability scans, penetration tests, and system and network monitoring to protect against and detect suspicious activity and potential data breaches. Firms must revise their security frameworks and lay down stringent security protocols to ensure the protection of client data and confidentiality. Regular security audits, vulnerability assessments, and employee training are also essential components of a robust cybersecurity strategy.

2. *Defend the Network Perimeter:* This involves routinely monitoring and testing security controls. Firms should employ secure configurations and ongoing security patch management for operating systems, applications and network devices, as well as monitoring for cybersecurity risk alerts.

3. *Restrict Access to Data:* Strictly control employees' access to confidential and sensitive information. Employees should only be given the minimum level of access in order to perform the requirements of their respective duty.

4. *Manage Passwords and User Privileges:* Review users' password and privileges policies. A strong password consists of at least 12 to 14 characters. Additionally, the password should include a combination of letters, numbers, and symbols. Law firms should implement the use of multi-factor authentication where feasible and appropriate.

5. *Backup System:* Develop a reliable backup strategy where the firm's data can easily be recovered in order to maintain business continuity. All backups should be stored offline and encrypted with a user-defined encryption key, whether on site, off site or stored in the cloud.

6. *Conduct Security Awareness Training for Employees:* Provide training and education to employees so that they are

aware of the law firm's security protocols and responsibility to protect a client's sensitive, confidential information. Law firms should conduct regular employee training and awareness programs to educate employees about security best practices, phishing guidelines, data policies, and procedures. They should provide mandatory cybersecurity awareness training to all users at least once a year. Regular training sessions ensure that attorneys and staff know how to identify phishing emails and scam attempts and report suspicious activity to IT personnel. Foster a culture where cybersecurity is everyone's responsibility. Encourage reporting of suspicious activities without fear of reprisal.

7. *Use Encryption for Transmitting Sensitive Data:* Encryption is the process of changing information in such a way as to make it unreadable by anyone except those possessing special knowledge that allows them to change the information back to its original, readable form. Use data encryption to protect data both at rest (stored data) and in transit (data being transmitted over networks).

8. *Third-Party Vendor Management:* Third-party vendors are one of the biggest security threats to any organization. Therefore, law firms should vet every vendor who works with the firm to ensure they exercise the same security protection as your firm. Law firms should carefully review vendor agreements for issues regarding indemnification, cyber liability insurance, and time periods for providing notice of vendor's "incident" or "breach."

9. *Establish an Incident Response Plan and Team:* Create and implement an incident response plan (IRP) and team (IRT) to be prepared to quickly contain, assess, and respond to a data security incident. Law firms should have a cross-organizational IRT in place, which includes not only management, but legal, human resources, procurement, finance, and IT to develop and implement a plan for detecting and managing a breach.

10. *Purchase a Standalone Cyber Liability Insurance Policy:* Examine all insurance policies in place for cyber coverage and consider purchasing a standalone cyber liability policy to cover first and third-party losses.

11. *Robust Technology Policies:* Clear and documented policies on technology use and security are the primary cybersecurity considerations for law firms. These policies provide a framework for managing technology-related risks. Clear and documented policies on technology use and security help law firms to mitigate risks, protect sensitive client data, ensure compliance with regulations, and guide employee behavior.

12. *Use of Firewall:* Firewalls are a primary tool your company can use to prevent malicious actors from accessing your systems. If you work from home or share a physical office with other lawyers in a different firm, then you should have a firewall and use the firewall to separate your networks into separate virtual local area networks (vLAN). A firewall is a device or program that controls the flow of network traffic between two networks or a device and a network that employ differing security posture.

10.5 CYBERSECURITY ATTORNEY

Recent surveys reveal that one of the top concerns for general counsel at private companies is cybersecurity. There is a need to build a cybersecurity practice within a law firm. It is in the company's strong interest to see the discipline of cybersecurity law develop and mature. The cybersecurity attorney must have a strong role within the company. They attorney must be a part of the operational team and needs a firm understanding of privacy law. A cybersecurity attorney must establish a strong base in foundational cybersecurity statutes in order to contribute effectively to the company's operations. An effective cybersecurity attorney has to be in the trenches, helping to develop the statements of work for new contracts, negotiating information-sharing agreements, advising on legal risks associated with the many and varied daily decisions of securing networks, and managing the hour-by-hour response during an incident. The attorney must be a key player in responding to cybersecurity incidents. Figure 10.9 illustrates a cybersecurity attorney [19].

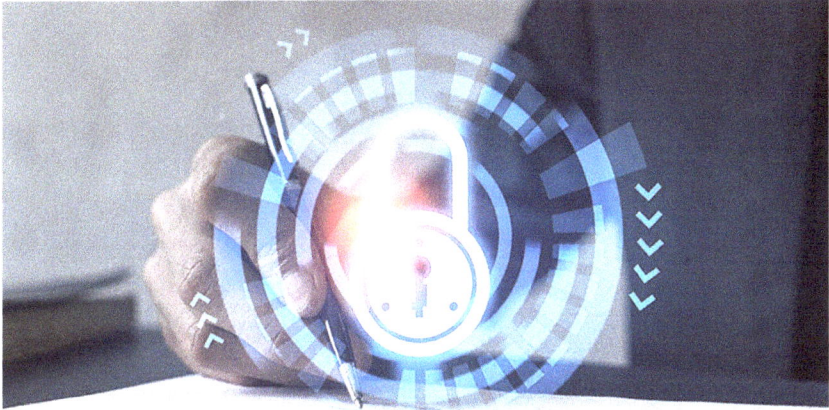

Figure 10.9 A cybersecurity attorney [19].

In addition, a cybersecurity attorney must also be aware of emerging legislation. The attorney should be able to help the company build relationships with key government agencies. The attorney must be multilingual in the jargon of both law and tech. One of the key jobs of such an attorney is to translate legal requirements (such as obligations imposed by regulations) into design requirements and to understand the technical details enough to ask probing questions, spot legal issues, and translate risks to organizational leadership. Much of the cybersecurity attorney's responsibility will involve decisions around avoiding, mitigating or accepting risk [20].

Modern cybersecurity experts must be well-versed in their understanding of privacy law and cyber law, which are actually two distinct branches of legal studies. Cyber law tends to be more concerned with broader rules and regulations related to the use of web-enabled devices. Privacy law, on the other hand, is more focused on a person's rights regarding the collection, storing, and sharing of their information. Cyber laws are the laws that provide legal protection to Internet users against a multitude of complexities and legal issues emerging every now and then. In addition to cyber laws at the federal level, it is also worth noting that 47 states have passed their own specific cybersecurity laws—with topics ranging from data privacy to breach notification.

10.6 BENEFITS

The impact of security breach is too large and too deep to allow any slip with respect to security preparedness. The consequences of data breach are severe. It includes financial losses, damage to reputation, legal liabilities, and loss of client trust. Law firm data security should be a top priority for any legal practice because clients trust you with their most confidential information. Data security failures can also have incredibly negative consequences for your clients. Cybersecurity has therefore become an essential part of legal practice management. Other benefits of cybersecurity include the following [21,22]:

• *Cloud Storage:* A common type of cloud service is cloud storage. Using a cloud service (as opposed to storing data on your own server or hard drive) may be an ideal security option for small-firm practitioners. Cloud storage is a simple way to store, access, and share data over the Internet. In other words, it is a method of storing data electronically so that the data is accessible anytime, from anywhere. When you use a cloud-storage service, instead of using your computer's hard drive or a networked server that you have to maintain, you pay a company to store that data on its servers. Provided you are selecting a vendor with adequate security practices, cloud storage is an excellent way to improve your efficiency and ensure that you are protecting files from inadvertent destruction.

• *Restricting Remote Access:* One of the appealing features of cloud services is that you can access your data from anywhere with an Internet connection. Cloud services also make it easy to collaborate with your co-workers and share files externally. Because cloud services make it easier for you to access data from anywhere, it also becomes easier for a third party to access your data from their own device. Although the ability to access information from anywhere gives you greater flexibility, it may cause you to expose client information.

• *Requiring Two-Factor Authentication:* One security strategy is protecting the login process with two-factor authentication. This requires two or more methods of verification before access is permitted. No matter how strong your password is, it can still be hacked. Adding two-factor authentication—which requires your password (the first factor) and a temporary code sent to another device (the second factor)—makes it that much more difficult for someone to access your device. In other words, two-factor authentication means you have to (1) enter your password, and (2) verify your identify by doing something like answering a secret question, or entering a code that is texted to your phone.

• *Limiting BYOD at Work:* Besides your own devices, if you have employees you also need to consider what devices they are bringing to work, and what devices they are using to review or access firm data. Your employment agreement should set out guidelines for staff.

• *Updating Software:* Out-of-date software is a hacker's dream. Keep the installation of your software and your operating systems really up to date. In essence, you are patching up possible security gaps in your software each time you update it. This decreases the chances of compromise of your information. Whether you are using a computer that runs Windows, Apple, or even Android, you can set your computer to allow for automatic updating, generally overnight.

• *Educating Your Clients:* Clients can still leave your firm vulnerable to cyberattacks despite your best efforts. Therefore, it is vital that you educate your clients on the latest trends and digital threats facing the legal industry. Notifying your clients about phishing attempts, ransomware, and other looming cyer threats can keep them from falling victim to hackers' deceptive attempts to steal their data.

• *Legal Obligations:* Non-compliance with these regulations not only exposes law firms to legal consequences but also undermines the reputation and credibility of the entire legal profession. Cybersecurity measures, therefore, become imperative to ensure compliance with regulatory standards and legal obligations.

• *Fraud:* Cyber laws are there to protect consumers from online frauds. They exist to prevent online crimes including credit card theft and identity theft. A person who commits such thefts stands to face federal and state criminal charges.

• *Copyright:* Copyright is a legal area that defends the rights of an entity be it an individual and/or a company to profit from their creative work. Individuals and companies both need copyright laws to prevent copyright infringement and enforce copyright protection.

• *Maintaining Operational Continuity:* Cybersecurity is not just about preventing unauthorized access; it also plays a crucial role in maintaining operational continuity. Ransomware attacks, for example, can paralyze law firms by encrypting essential data and demanding hefty ransoms for its release. Investing in cybersecurity measures, including regular backups and recovery plans, is essential to ensure that legal professionals can continue their work uninterrupted in the face of potential cyber threats.

• *24/7/365 Monitoring:* While up-to-date anti-virus and anti-malware software and firewalls are critical to security, they will not stop every threat. These protections must be supplemented with 24/7/365 monitoring of your entire system to identify unusual activity that could indicate an attack has occurred or is underway. Round-the-clock monitoring must be accompanied by a breach response plan to ensure rapid response to thwart potential attacks and limit any damage.

10.7 CHALLENGES

A lack of technological competency poses great cyber risks to data breaches and misuse. Working in cybersecurity law will require specialized education. Sometimes, companies have a poor cyber defense posture due to a lack of substantive knowledge about cybersecurity. Small firms are not immune to cyber attacks and are particularly at risk of impersonation fraud and business email compromise. Other challenges include [23]:

• *Skills Gap:* Cybersecurity law professionals are in high demand. From security analysts to pen testers, the need for employees trained and qualified in this field far outstrips the current supply. This skills gap includes people who hold a cybersecurity law degree. A common route to a job in cybersecurity law is to obtain a J.D. (Doctor of Jurisprudence) and pass the state bar exam. The need to understand and adhere to new and changing laws and regulations creates a thriving market for cybersecurity legal expertise.

• *Reputation:* For law firms, it is not just about the quality of legal services provided; it is about the trust and confidence clients place in them to handle sensitive information and navigate complex legal matters. Cyberattacks or breaches of client data can significantly tarnish a firm's reputation, leading to loss of clients, legal liabilities, and financial losses.

• *Regulation Compliance:* Legal firms are subject to various regulatory requirements. Cybersecurity regulation compliance is crucial to business success. It is a critical concern for law firms in today's digital landscape. Law firms are prime targets for cyber-attacks as highly sensitive client information custodian. A cybersecurity attorney needs to understand the regulatory landscape. Various regulations, like the General Data Protection Regulation (GDPR) in the EU and state-specific laws in the US, mandate strict data security measures. Regular updates, training, and compliance checks are crucial to safeguarding the sensitive information that is the bedrock of the legal profession.

• *Government:* In cybersecurity, companies must expect to engage with government. This is inevitable. A cybersecurity attorney must understand the delineation of each government agency's authorities. Government lawyers often seek to negotiate novel public-private arrangements that benefit both the company and the larger ecosystem.

• *Ethical Concern:* Be aware of your ethical and legal obligations, including ABA Ethics Opinions and state data protection laws. As an entity that collects, manages, stores, and interacts with confidential information, your law firm has a moral, ethical, and legal responsibility to its clients. Specifically, you must proactively work to maintain the security and integrity of sensitive data.

10.8 CONCLUSION

Cyberattacks have unfortunately become part of the environment for businesses and other organizations. Since law firms handle large volumes of sensitive data, the cybersecurity risk is significantly more present than ever. The importance of cybersecurity and data protection in the legal profession cannot be overstated. The journey towards robust cybersecurity and data protection is ongoing, evolving with technological advancements and emerging threats. The practice of cybersecurity law is still very much in the early stages. Law firms' cybersecurity environment is expected to undergo continuous change as cyber threats are anticipated to emerge.

Prioritizing cybersecurity can provide a competitive edge for a law firm. In today's digital age, clients are increasingly concerned about the security of their personal information. By adhering to strict data protection practices, we can attract clients who value privacy and data security, setting ourselves apart from competitors in the legal industry. As a legal practitioner, your goal should not only be to respond to a cyberattack, but also to actively prepare for one. By taking proactive steps, you can significantly reduce the risk of a cyberattack and ensure that your data remains secure. More information on cybersecurity in the legal practice can be found in the books in [24-33] and the following related journal: *Law Society Journal.*

REFERENCE

[1] "Why is cyber security important in the construction industry?" August 2024,

https://k3techs.com/why-is-cyber-security-important-in-the-construction-industry/#:~:text=Protecting%20Your%20Projects%20from%20Digital%20Threats&text=Any%20breach%20can%20lead%20to,essential%20to%20protect%20valuable%20data.&text=Therefore%2C%20it%20is%20crucial%20for,invest%20in%20robust%20cybersecurity%20measures.

[2] M. N. O. Sadiku, P. A. Adekunte, and J. O. Sadiku, "Cybersecurity in the legal industry," *International Journal of Trend in Scientific Research and Development*, vol. 9, no. 2, March-April 2025, pp. 861-872.

[3] P. Singh, "A layered approach to cybersecurity: People, processes, and technology- explored & explained," July 2021,

https://www.linkedin.com/pulse/layered-approach-cybersecurity-people-processes-singh-casp-cisc-ces

[4] M. Loi et al., "Cybersecurity in health – disentangling value tensions," *Journal of Information, Communication and Ethics in Society*, June 2019,

https://www.emerald.com/insight/content/doi/10.1108/JICES-12-2018-0095/full/html

[5] M. Adams, "Unlocking the benefits of ethical hacking: The importance of ethical hackers in cybersecurity," April 2023,

https://www.businesstechweekly.com/cybersecurity/network-security/ethical-hacking/

[6] M. N. O. Sadiku, S. Alam, S. M. Musa, and C. M. Akujuobi, "A primer on cybersecurity," *International Journal of Advances in Scientific Research and Engineering*, vol. 3, no. 8, Sept. 2017, pp. 71-74.

[7] M. N. O. Sadiku, M. Tembely, and S. M. Musa, "Smart grid cybersecurity," *Journal of Multidisciplinary Engineering Science and Technology*, vol. 3, no. 9, September 2016, pp.5574-5576.

[8] "FCC Small Biz Cyber Planning Guide,"

https://transition.fcc.gov/cyber/cyberplanner.pdf

[9] "The 8 most common cybersecurity attacks to be aware of,"

https://edafio.com/blog/the-8-most-common-cybersecurity-attacks-to-be-aware-of/

[10] Y. Li and Q. Liu, "A comprehensive review study of cyber-attacks and cyber security; Emerging trends and recent developments," *Energy Reports*, vol. 7, November 2021,

https://www.sciencedirect.com/science/article/pii/S2352484721007289

[11] Y. Zhang, "Cybersecurity and reliability of electric power grids in an interdependent cyber-physical environment," *Doctoral Dissertation*, University of Toledo, 2015.

[12] E. Baxter and A. Haslam, "Cybersecurity and legal regulation: Why it's crucial to stay on top of cyber risk," September 2024,

https://lsj.com.au/articles/cybersecurity-and-legal-regulation-why-its-crucial-to-stay-on-top-of-cyber-risk/

[13] A. Sharma, "Cybersecurity and its growing importance in law firms," July 2024,

https://www.a3logics.com/blog/cybersecurity-for-law-firms/

[14] "The top 5 cybersecurity risks for law firms," October 2024,

https://uptimepractice.com/cybersecurity-risks-for-law-firms/

[15] "Cybersecurity Legal," February 2024,

https://www.legalprod.com/en/cybersecurity-legal/

[16] "Safeguarding justice: The critical role of cybersecurity within your legal practice"

https://www.orca.co.uk/safeguarding-justice-the-critical-role-of-cybersecurity-within-your-legal-practice/

[17] "Cyber security: A lawyer's guide to data protection," June 2023,

https://insight.thomsonreuters.com/mena/legal/posts/cyber-security-a-lawyers-guide-to-data-protection

[18] "11 Best cybersecurity practices to protect your firm,"

https://sc.edu/study/colleges_schools/law/about/news/2020/11_best_cybersecurity_practices.php

[19] R. Kaushal, "Cybersecurity for law firms: What legal professionals should know," November 2024,

https://www.legalsupportworld.com/blog/cybersecurity-for-law-firms/

[20] D. Sutherland, "What is a cybersecurity legal practice?" April 2021,

https://www.lawfaremedia.org/article/what-cybersecurity-legal-practice

[21] "Cybersecurity guide," October 2021,

https://www.wsba.org/for-legal-professionals/member-support/practice-management-assistance/guides/cybersecurity-guide

[22] "The role of cyber law in cybersecurity,"

https://www.eccu.edu/blog/cybersecurity/the-role-of-cyber-laws-in-cybersecurity/

[23] S. Bowcut, "From JD to cyber pro: Your cybersecurity law degree roadmap," December 2024,

https://cybersecurityguide.org/programs/cybersecurity-law/

[24] M. N. O. Sadiku, *Cybersecurity and Its Applications*. Moldova, Europe: Lambert Academic Publishing, 2023.

[25] J. Rhodes, R. Litt, P. S. Rosenzweig (eds.), *The ABA*

Cybersecurity Handbook: A Resource for Attorneys, Law Firms, and Business Professionals. American Bar Association, 3rd edition, 2022.

[26] C. J. Hoofnagle, and G. G. Richard III, *Cybersecurity in Context: Technology, Policy, and Law*. Wiley, 2024.

[27] E. Duby, *Raising the Bar on Cybersecurity: What Law Firms Need To Know To Securely Navigate Today's Technology Risks*. Independently Published, 2025.

[28] I. Priyadarshini and C. Cotton, *Cybersecurity: Ethics, Legal, Risks, and Policies*. Apple Academic Press, 2024.

[29] N. Babazadeh, *Legal Ethics And Cybersecurity: Managing Client Confidentiality In The Digital Age: Journal of Law and Cyber Warfare*. Independently Published, 2020.

[30] F. Bergamasco, R. Cassar, and R. Popova, *Cybersecurity: Key Legal Considerations for the Aviation and Space Sectors*. Wolters Kluwer, 2020.

[31] G. Siboni and L. Ezioni (eds.), *Cybersecurity And Legal-regulatory Aspects*. World Scientific Publishing Company, 2021.

[32] J. Kosseff, *Cybersecurity Law*. Wiley, 2017.

[33] C. A. Tschider, *International Cybersecurity and Privacy Law in Practice*. Wolters Kluwer, 2nd Edition, 2023.

INDEX

www.ingramcontent.com/pod-product-compliance
Lightning Source LLC
Chambersburg PA
CBHW040851210326
41597CB00029B/4797